AMERICAN BIOGRAPHY:
ITS THEORY AND PRACTICE

American Biography

Its Theory and Practice

CT34
.U6
M57

70997

DANA KINSMAN MERRILL

THE BOWKER PRESS
PORTLAND, MAINE

Library of Congress Catalogue Card Number 57-9961

PRINTED IN THE UNITED STATES OF AMERICA

TO THE MEMORY OF

KATHERINE RAWLEY MERRILL

PREFACE

In this book I have undertaken to examine the nature of American biography from its beginnings in the Colonial time to the middle of the twentieth century. I have considered first the theory of the art and second its practice in the chronological order. To illustrate the essential character of biography from these two standpoints, I have chosen books which are representative of the motives, methods and workmanship of the different types of lives and the succeeding generations of biographers. My plan embraces the philosophical principles which the authors expressed or implied in their works and the technical principles of their craftsmanship. As the book is intended to be primarily a study of biography as a literary form, I have paid more attention to the biographers and their practice than to the personalities and careers of the figures they portrayed.

I am well aware that in my selection of representative biographies works as worthy and as deficient as those chosen have been omitted. The selection of a limited number of examples in a field in which thousands of volumes have been produced can not be absolute, or meet with unanimous agreement, but I believe that the specimens cited here adequately exemplify objective life-writing in its main types and techniques. I have devoted considerable attention to the lives of Lincoln for the reason that a line of biographies of a single great character is an excellent index to the changing modes of life-writing.

My study has been confined to life-writing in its objective sense, that is, lives written or compiled by persons other than the men and women depicted. The subjective forms of autobiography, diary, personal journal and letter, significant as these records are in their own categories, have not been within the scope of my purpose. They are considered only briefly and in certain cases where they were used as source-material by biographers. *American biography* has been defined as all objective life-literature written by American authors whether their subjects were American or not.

Through the vast area of American biography there are highways and byways which remain to be developed. This examination of the field aims, as has been said, to set forth the theory and the practice of an art which records human individuality of every kind and human activity in every sphere.   DANA K. MERRILL

ACKNOWLEDGMENTS

I wish to thank the following for their permissions to use certain quotations in this book: Paul M. Angle, Catherine Drinker Bowen, Marchette Chute, Henry Steele Commager, Waldo H. Dunn, Howard Mumford Jones and William Schuman. Also the editors of *The Atlantic Monthly, The Musical Quarterly, The New England Quarterly, The New York Times Book Review* and *The Saturday Review*. Also Appleton-Century-Crofts, Inc. for a passage from *Biography: The Literature of Personality;* E. P. Dutton & Company, Inc. for quotations from *English Biography* and *Shakespeare of London;* Harcourt, Brace and Company, Inc. for a passage from *Eminent Victorians;* Little, Brown & Company for a passage from *John Adams and the American Revolution;* Rutgers University Press for a quotation from *The Lincoln Reader.* Further acknowledgment is made with each quotation.

CONTENTS

COMMENTARY

All things are engaged in writing their particular history.—RALPH WALDO EMERSON

It is indecorous—and perilous—to pry into your neighbor's private affairs. But it is widely regarded as distinguished scholarship to pry into the most intimate secrets of departed celebrities. Under that peculiar convention's beneficent authority, the art of biography flourishes.—CHARLES POORE

Biography is the only true historical record of human nature, for this is the history of spiritual causes, of which physical changes—all the vicissitudes of external life—are but the consequences.—AMOS BRONSON ALCOTT

When life is framed in death the picture is ready to hang.—HENRY JAMES

To make a perfect biography, a man's self-knowledge ought to be united to a stranger's calm, impartial, disinterested judgment—a thing not likely to be seen on earth.—PHILLIPS BROOKS

AMERICAN BIOGRAPHY:
ITS THEORY AND PRACTICE

Book I: THE THEORY OF AMERICAN BIOGRAPHY

CHAPTER I

THE NATURE OF BIOGRAPHY

The secure place which biography holds in American culture is founded on the universality of the subject and its enduring appeal. The human individual in all his aspects is the concern of biography. His nature and its manifestations, his interests and activities, whether he is at work or at play, his endeavors, whether he succeeds or fails, his relations with others—these are the things which biography investigates and records.

Whatever is his status in society, every human being is the possible hero—or the victim—of a written life. Few actual persons appear by name in poetry or the novel or the drama, and formal history presents the public side—but not the private affairs—of comparatively few men and women. Everyone is a potential object of the biographer's attention: anyone may benefit from the talent of a skillful and intelligent author; no one is safe from the folly of an incompetent or inimical writer. In its portrayal of actual persons and the unlimited range of its potential characters, biography occupies a unique place among literary forms.

Biographers have chosen their figures from every race and social class, from every vocation and profession, from every sphere of activity in which men and women have become famous or notorious. Nor is biography confined to the celebrated and the known. Not a few obscure and inglorious characters have been depicted by authors who recognized their biographical worth. If the statement is true that democracy levels all men, biography raises them to the distinction of the printed page, and a library of life-literature brings them together in an order that is both appropriate and incongruous. On the shelves of the library the life of John C. Calhoun stands in queer propinquity to the career of Al Capone. The saga of P. T. Barnum adjoins the life of Clara Barton. Thomas Jefferson and Jesse James are neighbors on the shelf, as are Harriet Beecher Stowe and John L. Sullivan. Among the rows of other volumes presidents and "also rans," patriot and traitor, believer and agnostic, capitalist and Communist, law-maker and law-breaker, native and immigrant, plebeian and aristocrat—all these, as well as individuals in other categories, rub biographical elbows, as it were, regardless of their careers in actual existence.

"The basis of biography is the identity of human life and human nature. If we were all fundamentally different, we should take little interest in each other's actions and motives, because we should be quite incapable of entering into them and understanding them. With all the superficial diversity, human beings at large are like each other. The same passions drive us, the same fears restrain us, the same long, undying ambitions urge us on to ever renewed achievement, and the same fatal weariness and despair at times overcome us, only to give place to hope reborn and the ever varied, unfailing effort to accomplish something, often we know not what . . .

"After grasping this fundamental identity of humanity, we then come to understand the interest of the superficial differences. If all men were different, we should not care to study them, nor should we if they were all absolutely alike. There is the common basis of general traits of character, but these traits are modified in every particular case with the infinite play of complexity which makes the study of them as endlessly difficult as it is fascinating."[1]

II

The word *biography* in its simplest sense means the life history of a human being. Much is implicit in this nuclear definition: the professional equipment of the biographer, the materials he uses, the method of his treatment, and the structure and content of the completed work. A conclusive answer to the question of what biography is must take into consideration the varying lengths of life-accounts, the different forms in which biographies are cast, and the philosophical and technical principles of the authors.

A narrative of a person's life may be limited to a few hundred words, it may run into several large volumes, or it may fall in length anywhere between these two extremes. In the matter of types, one kind of narrative is confined to the character and career of an individual; another kind is widened to embrace the background of the individual's time; a third type of narrative is freely interspersed with letters which he wrote and received; a fourth kind is written in the form of a novel. Still another form may include a critical study of its figure's achievement in literature, music or painting. A treatment of a life may even disregard the

[1] Foreword "The Significance of Biography" by Gamaliel Bradford in James C. Johnston, *Biography: The Literature of Personality*, pp. xv-xvii.

time-order of events and set forth the hero in topical form. Each one of these works, regardless of its length and the nature and organization of its contents, is a biography within the meaning of the term. All these species have not, of course, existed fully shaped from the beginnings of American life-literature in the Colonial time. They evolved as the original biographical form developed through the years.

In its specific features and texture biography has not meant the same thing in all generations. Craftsmen in the field have differed on the questions of what should go into the personal history and how the history should be written. Modes and patterns have varied, not only from time to time, but also within the limits of any one period. Every "dominant trend" and "prevailing fashion" has had its exceptions and opposites. This diversity in practice and product has been inevitable. The basic principles of biography have felt the force of changing philosophies, and they have been put to use by biographers of every temperament and school. American biography, then, is a body of heterogeneous life-writing whose nature must be examined in the line of its tradition as well as in the light of its separate periods.

In the broad meaning of the word, the literature of biography contains two general divisions: the autobiographical, in which the central character tells his own story, and the objective, in which the figure is set forth by another person. In common use the term *biography* refers only to objective works. The two divisions resemble each other to a large extent, but the basic difference in point of view which exists between an autobiographer and a biographer is reflected in the choice and presentation of their material and in the interpretation of their data.

Biography, being a record of the past created with the apparatus of literature, is a compound made up chiefly of historical and literary elements, and as such it is directly related to history and literature. Biography, however, has evolved definite principles of its own. It is governed by established techniques. It combines the procedures of both science and art. It is an entity in itself.[2]

Biography is that branch of writing whose function is to re-create the individuality and the life of an actual man or woman. *Individuality* is the sum of the characteristics which distinguish the figure as a specific human being. It comprises the distinctive spiritual, moral and mental qualities which determine personality and character. *Life* is the sequence of the experiences of the person. A book of biography thus becomes a record of inner workings and external manifestations. These two sides of the figure are depicted in varying degrees by different biographers. "The subtle mysteries and secret of personality" may form the absorbing study of one author and be a lesser interest to another, who devotes his chief attention to outward actions. Whatever the proportion of the two parts, however, the heart of a work of biography is the revelation of an individuality.

Therein lies the primary appeal of biography. It is a kind of characterization and concentrates its attention on the qualities and actions which distinguish the individuality of its figures. Yet if it were only an analysis of character and nothing more, biography would have but a limited in-

---

[2]The stage of development which American life-writing reached in the first quarter of the twentieth century led to the assertion that biography did not achieve the status of an art until that time. This was not the case. Biography was an art as soon as it became a deliberate creative activity in a circumscribed field and was governed by recognized principles. This evolution was a gradual process, and it was consummated by the middle of the nineteenth century. In a critical essay printed in the *North American Review* in March, 1818, (Vol. VI, p. 293) Jared Sparks described the duty of biographers and the requisite qualities of a satisfying biography. Both Sparks and Washington Irving demonstrated biography as an art before 1850. If many works of the earlier nineteenth century fall considerably below the later standards, their inferiority does not negate the existence of the art status.

terest. Life-writing usually takes the shape of narrative, and the human nature it reveals is unfolded in the form of a story. As the course of man's existence never runs smooth, the hero contends with obstacles on his road and with conflicts in his soul. The play of opposing forces in his life gives to the biography the element of "plot" and dramatic struggle.

Man's curiosity about man has been marked in the twentieth century by an eagerness to know the reasons for human behavior. The "invisible life" of biographical subjects —the springs of their actions and the motives of their conduct—has been searched and explained, intelligently and absurdly, by many investigators. Thus the interpretative element, which is common to all biography, has expanded. Some authors pass judgment on their figures, evaluating the traits of the subjects, justifying or censuring their acts, appraising their achievements, and suggesting if not defining the place of the figures in their field of activity. In biographies of this kind, criticism is added to interpretation.

All life-literature is not composed by the pattern that was outlined in the preceding paragraphs, but every work contains those ingredients in selective combinations and varying proportions. In terms of a formula, biography is made up of elements that are analytic, descriptive, narrative, explanatory, interpretative and critical. Any one of these elements, when it is properly used, affords the reader some knowledge of a man or woman. Collectively, they touch every side of an individual and his existence. They furnish answers to the questions which readers of biography have more or less consciously in mind.

The three cardinal virtues of a superior biography are its truth, vitality and style. Through the first the portrait and narrative are in literal and spiritual agreement with the original character and career. Though the second the story of the hero and his experiences is vibrant with the force and movement of actual life. The chronicle is re-created reality in natural motion. It is not hard to assemble facts and prove that a man lived. It is no easy task to bring him to biographical life exactly as he did live. Through style the biography exhibits a manner of expression which not only represents "a perfect mutual understanding between the worker and his material," but is also in harmony with the individuality and acts of the person who is being portrayed.

Style is the factor which more often tips the scales for or against a biography, in the mind of the reader. Style makes the book read, it aids the reader to understand the hero better, it adds to his pleasure. Style is the final test of the biographer's artistry. It is often the deciding quality in the reader's assessment of the book. The narrative may be accurate and honest, it may acquaint the reader clearly and fully with the subject; but if the writer's manner of expression is deficient, the biography suffers a serious handicap. An inferior style not only turns readers away and lessens the pleasure of those who toil through the pages, it also inflicts an unwarranted penalty on the figure. Any hero or villain, regardless of his personal excellence or wickedness, is entitled to stylistic justice in the court of life-literature. An adequate or superior style fortifies the truth and strengthens the vitality of the biography.

To satisfy the demands of its art, a biography should have all three of the prime requisites. One or two of them are not sufficient. A chronicle may be truthful down to the last detail and yet lack vitality and a felicitous style. It may be lively enough to arouse the most jaded mind and be false to the human life it depicts. An engaging style adds to the vitality of the narrative, but it sheds no light on the truth or error of the subject matter.

III

The basic commodity of biography is fact. That the biographer's first and greatest concern should be the truth is axiomatic. Truth is conformity to fact. The foundation of the art is authenticity. A false biography is worthless. A work that manipulates its fact to aid or hurt its figure loses proportionately in its value. A patient reader makes allowance for an unskilled style or a dull recital of details, or even for judgments of the author that stir his dissent, but he can not forgive a presentation which deliberately departs from the truth of the original life. Whether a reader prefers an objective narrative that lacks the author's opinions, whether he chooses a rendering that is seasoned with critical interpretation, or whether he relishes a personal history that is cast in the novelized form, the lover of biography desires to feel that he is getting the essential truth in the book before him. No one is on record with the demand for a biography that does not tell the truth.

Truth in the biographical sense is what the figure was in reality, what he thought and said and did; it is the sum of all the distinguishing characteristics, actions and happenings that serve to identify him and his life. The principle of truth is easily stated. The search for the concrete thing is a task of infinite magnitude.

Even if the truth has been established, it is not always easily discovered. Truth does not always lie in a white light, nor is it invariably stamped with its unmistakable earmark. Men and women do not order their lives for the convenience of future chroniclers, nor do they simplify the complexities of their existence for the benefit of later investigators. Time and again they resemble the poets who leave enigmatical passages in their verses. Many segments of the records of every career are factually clear, definite and incontestable. Other parts are missing or confused or open to conjecture. The preciousness of truth may be a reason for its elusiveness.

Adherence to the truth, when that sovereign thing can be found, would seem to be the easiest part of the author's undertaking. Biographers without end have proclaimed their fidelity to their subjects. Scores of them have faithfully reproduced the record as they found it. Others have regarded the truth, not in the face of reality, but in the light of their personal convictions or in their purpose in writing. Among this number are those who believe that a particular man has been over- or under-estimated in the works of previous authors, and those who think that the "true character" or the "real achievement" of a certain personage has not been rightly explained. Not a few superior biographies have been written out of convictions of this nature. In these cases, however, the convictions of the authors were amply supported by the demonstrable facts; the persuasions which preceded the study of the man were not used to distort or misrepresent the facts. Some biographers have found the "truth" in their own fondness for or in their antipathy to their figure by reason of his personal qualities, his political principles, or some aspect of his career. Still other authors have shaped the truth according to the fashions of the time in which they wrote. In some instances authors have seemed to believe that the essence of truth lay within themselves rather than in the records and individualities of their subjects.

The difficulty—or the impossibility—of ascertaining the biographical truth has been variously pointed out.

Emily Dickinson wrote tersely: "Biography first convinces us of the fleeing of the biographied." Yet biographic victims do not always escape the hunter. They do not all present a common front to those who pursue them. Rather, they concur or submit; they elude or baffle; they defy or mock; they enthrall or rule; they even deceive or in part defeat the biographer.

Walt Whitman said to his friend Horace Traubel: "While I accept the records I think we know very little of the actual. I often reflect, how very different every fellow must have been from the fellow we come upon in the myths—with the surroundings, the incidents, the push and pull of the concrete moment, all left out or wrongly set forth. It is hard to extract a man's real self—any man—from such a chaotic mass—from such historic débris."

Gamaliel Bradford, a biographer himself, speaks of the "secret of personality, which always teases us and always eludes us just when it seems most firmly within our grasp."

William Dean Howells thought of writing an autobiography, saying that "it would forestall a biography, always a false and mistaken thing." Whether this was a casual opinion or whether Howells always held that view of biography is a question.

Esther Forbes, author of a life of Paul Revere, told an interviewer: "No matter how hard the biographer works, those innermost secrets, with which the novelist starts, are forever unsolved."

E. A. Robinson once defined poetry as a language that tells us something that can not be said. From a similar point of view, biography might be termed an art which re-creates that which can not be restored. Readers may well agree that a life is skillfully or poorly written, but the fidelity of biographies is constantly a moot point. The ideal can only be striven for, but the quest is a fascinating endeavor.

IV

The elementary function of biography is to re-create a life as it was lived and to make clear an individuality as it was constituted. This function is basic, absolute and timeless. It derives its validity from the ideal of Truth to which the creative instinct aspires. Whether observed or not, the law remains constant. Its validity is not impaired by the changing fashions of the times or by the dicta of critics.

Biographers of every generation in this country have by their own testimony been aware of the principle, even though they ignored its implications. They were conscious of the obligation they assumed, and with comparatively few exceptions each one of them may have believed that he was performing his duty, however short of the goal his completed work may have been. In actual practice they altered the elementary function of the art and made biography serve other purposes as well. Innumerable authors adopted the roles of moralist, teacher, hero-worshipper, guardian or assailant of reputations, custodian of dignity, reformer and stump speaker. American life-literature thus contains in its volumes that were written deliberately from those standpoints a large admixture of eulogy, ethical teaching, dislike and hatred, sheer invention, propaganda political and other, and whatever else authors might wish to insert in their narratives.

These elements are the marks of "impure" biography. They are introduced by the author to serve a special purpose of his own. They are not found in the original lives and personalities of the figures in whose biographies they appear. Neither are they required in the service of interpretation. They fulfill no technical or artistic need. These adulterants have been the impedimenta of American life-literature. They have perverted the true function of the art, and they have obstructed the genuine re-creation of men and women.

The use of these things has been upheld—more tacitly than audibly—as a right inherent in the biographic process. That an author should have the privilege to defend his hero against the charges of critics is a just prerogative. That he should enjoy the freedom to give temperate praise to his figure can hardly be denied. That he should make a worthy life a lesson in spiritual or material achievement may be granted. These instances presuppose that no harm is done to the primary function of biography. Times without end, however, biographers have neglected the basic aim in the interest of their special purposes.

Extraneous elements not only weaken the essential substance of a biography, they also make the judicious reader question the accuracy and completeness of the picture before him. The author is under suspicion, and his narrative does not receive unqualified acceptance. Less critical readers take other attitudes toward impure biographies. Warm admirers of a biographic figure are likely to welcome the applause which the author bestows on their hero. Partisans likewise hail propaganda which is on their side. Those who are sympathetic to the didactic accept the moralizing strain on their own terms. The indifferent reader does not object to invented matter if it does not distort the main lines of the portrait or detract from the pleasure of his reading.

Authors have not always marred their narratives in departing from the primary function of biography. In two instances they have expanded its purpose to excellent advantage. The life-and-times type of biography, which combines the hero's career with the relevant background of his period, is a needed form of personal history. The other form is the critical study, in which the author, besides narrating a person's life, evaluates the work of his subject in literature, painting, architecture or other field. These two types have legitimate places in biographical writing. The methods that are used, if they are handled competently, do not detract from the interpretation of the figure, nor do they make the reader skeptical of the whole biography.

Biography in its purest form combines the narrative of a life and the delineation of a character without extraneous purpose or matter of any kind. The author does not attempt to teach or to propagandize. He applies to his figure no whitewash or charcoal of his own making. He does not shape his work to support a thesis or to advance a cause. He invents no incidents or conversation, even if these are, allegedly, in harmony with the subject's career. The writer of the "pure" biography confines his work to the substance, spirit and tone of the original life. Having sought to set forth the man truthfully and accurately, he lets the finished product stand for itself. This conformity to reality, as far as that can be attained, renders its own praise or blame of the figure. It instructs or counsels or condemns in its own way. It is its own exemplar of what can be rightly derived from the life and character of the person portrayed. Pure biographies are not infallible, nor are they necessarily distinguished works. They must also be measured for their validity and value by other requisites. These will be considered in a later chapter.

CHAPTER II

WHY BIOGRAPHY IS WRITTEN AND READ

The motives to biographical writing are numerous and complicated. The instinct of curiosity is a strong element among the several forces which have operated to create life-literature. If some biographers have been impelled by a single aim, others have been actuated by a plural purpose. It would be futile to attempt to determine the specific motivation behind every work of biography, but the chief incentives to the practice are clear.

Oldest is the aim to commemorate. Biography in its primordial origin in the ancient world sprang from "an inherent and deep-seated desire in man to perpetuate the memory of a life." The earliest biographers among the English-speaking people in America—the clergymen of Massachusetts in the Colonial time—were stirred by the same desire. They were impressed by the characters and deeds of certain of their fellow-men, and they wrote their accounts in order to preserve the memory of these men. In the early years of the nation the same motive was strong in the hearts of the biographers who celebrated Washington and the other heroes of the Revolutionary Period. The commemorative purpose has continued to be a fundamental object of biographical writing, although the nature of the memorials has changed from time to time to meet the fashions and demands of different generations. Whatever motives may have been in the minds of the authors, later biographies which have the effect of being impressive memorials of their figures are *John Brown* (1910) by Oswald Garrison Villard, *Mark Twain* (1912) by Albert Bigelow Paine, *R. E. Lee* (1934, 1935) by Douglas Southall Freeman, *Benjamin Franklin* (1938) by Carl Van Doren, and *Abraham Lincoln: The Prairie Years* (1926) and *The War Years* (1939) by Carl Sandburg.

A second object of biography has been to teach—to set forth the example of a good life for the edification of the reader. In the memoirs of the Colonial time the didactic aim came to be a natural concomitant of commemorative purpose. A man who deserved to be remembered for his spiritual distinction and intellectual attainments was also worthy of being emulated by others. The moralizing element was conspicuous in the accounts of the early clergymen. The didactic strain continued, in a strong but lesser degree, through the first half of the nineteenth century. After that time the deliberate preceptive purpose declined in biographies written for adult readers. When it has been visible at all in the twentieth century, it has appeared more often by implication than as an avowed aim.

Many a biography has been written from the sheer interest which an author feels in a particular person. This interest often amounts to a fervor. The biography may be a work of art, or it may be only a document on a man or a "book" about a hero. In all these cases, however, the motive behind the biography is the same. The author feels an enthusiasm or a passion which impels him to the creative effort. The process that is involved in reconstructing an actual human life is highly provocative. It enables the biographer to study at close view the individuality and experiences of the figure who has drawn his interest. It challenges him to discover answers to the unsolved questions in the career of his subject. It summons him to re-create a hero or heroine in a true and artistic likeness. These conditions constitute one of the points of appeal which biography possesses.

The biographer Henry Steele Commager says that he wrote his life of Theodore Parker, a transcendentalist and a Unitarian minister of Boston, "because I could not help myself, and I have written it for my own satisfaction more than for the edification of others." Samuel Eliot Morison explains that his life of Columbus "arose out of a desire to know exactly where Columbus sailed on his Four Voyages, and what sort of seaman he was." Mr. Morison adds that "no previous work on the Discoverer of America answers these questions in a way to satisfy even an amateur seafarer." He obtained answers to the questions by voyaging some ten thousand miles in command of his own vessels, following the routes Columbus had taken, and visiting the places where the explorer had been.

The last biographical word on a compelling figure is never said. Even definitive lives do not end the making of new books about their heroes. As long as a man or a woman remains of sufficient interest to later generations, there always exists among biographers the desire to write their own personal interpretations of the individual in question. In some cases the authors do not deny the general fidelity of previous narratives of their subject; they simply want to draw their own portraits in their own way, according to their study and conclusions. More often, however, the leading motive of these authors is to modify or correct or improve upon earlier portrayals of their subject. Washington and Lincoln have been depicted in endless volumes. To a large but lesser extent Franklin and Jefferson, Grant and Lee, Melville and Whitman have engaged the attention of biographers.

This objective—to set forth the "true" man—is entertained by expert craftsmen as well as incompetent aspirants, and it consequently works both good and harm to the cause it attempts to serve. The motive produces excellent biographies which amply fulfill the aim of the authors, and it also spawns poorly conceived books. The latter at their best add nothing to previous interpretations; at their worst they spread false impressions of their figures.

The foregoing motives are those which have brought into existence the greater number of American biographies. Various other reasons have appeared in biographical writing, although these are not necessarily independent of the purposes which have just been discussed. The special or sudden prominence of popular figures, like Will Rogers and Knute Rockne, or men of the hour, as General Grant and General Eisenhower, quickly calls forth lives to meet the public interest. Scores of biographies have been published in national political campaigns to advance the fortunes of presidential candidates. Some biographies have been undertaken at the request of the subjects themselves or of their families. Others have been written on assignment by publishers or by editors who were planning new series of lives. No small number of biographies have been compiled as doctoral dissertations in graduate schools of universities.

II

The offer of biography to the reader is as broad and diverse as life itself. Without petition or formality he may make the immediate acquaintance of any man or woman whose life has been written. He meets the character on his own terms, as it were, and may read for the purpose which suits his fancy or desire, whether it be for pleasure or profit. He may terminate the acquaintance at will, if he and the character prove to be incompatible; or he may carry the relationship, if he wishes, into an extended study of the figure.

Along its shelves biography holds out to the reader the source of diversion and entertainment, of knowledge and wisdom, of sorrow and happiness, of anger and vexation, of solace and inspiration. It enables him to witness drama of his own choice—comedy or tragedy or any other transcript of human experience in which players from seemingly the whole cast of mankind re-enact the roles they created, lightly or seriously, easily or laboriously, in real life. Each book is like a private theatrical performance at which the reader is the sole spectator.

The lover of biography has endless opportunity to indulge his tastes and interests. He may sit at the councils of peace and war in the White House. He may stump the Illinois towns with Lincoln and Douglas, and witness political vengeance in the impeachment of Andrew Johnson. He may search for birds with Audubon in the forests, explore the wilderness with Lewis and Clark, and ride the Oregon trail with Parkman. He may watch the building of Brooklyn Bridge and "live deliberately" with Thoreau at Walden Pond. He may go on military campaigns with Grant, Lee and Eisenhower, and watch naval warfare with John Paul

Jones, Farragut and King. He may meet the members of famous families—the Adamses, the Lees, the Jameses and others—in their public and private lives, and he may make the acquaintance of John Gilley, the fisherman of the Maine coast.

Furthermore, the reader of biography may look on the research of Carver in peanuts and sweet potatoes, and he may see the birth of Edison's inventions. He may feel the emotional outburst which followed the publication of *Uncle Tom's Cabin,* and he may thrill at the crusades of Lucretia Mott. He may live not only in the world of Paul Revere, but also in the world of Jonathan Edwards, of Horace Greeley, of Edwin Forrest and of Charles W. Eliot. These random sidelights suggest only a few of the adventures which await the biographile.

The reader may take biography as he wishes. He may remain a purely objective observer of the characters and happenings before him, fully alive to the revelation of personality and the march of events, enjoying the performance, but not entering into the feelings of the actors or having an eye to any practical benefit for himself. Or he may participate vicariously in the life of the protagonist of the drama, responding sympathetically to the ups and downs of the latter's fortunes, and sharing the emotions and experiences of the hero. The reader may also let biography be a "friend and aider" to him in the business of living. A library of worthwhile volumes is a collection of case-histories in the problem of existence, a huge dossier of universal attributes and human affairs in which he will find a surprisingly large part of himself duplicated and catalogued under other names. The places, events and external circumstances are different from his own life, but there is a likeness between the inner things of the spirit. He learns the ways and means by which other individuals have travelled the common road, and the knowledge he gains from their lives he may turn to good account in meeting the changing fortunes of his own existence.

Biography has always been a potential source of self-knowledge to the reader. A widespread method of portraiture in the twentieth century has brought out this aspect of life-literature more strongly than ever before. Biographers who adopted the procedure showed a marked desire to explore the consciousness and behavior of their subjects. Unsatisfied with the narration of only external actions and visible circumstances, they sought causes, motives and reasons, and in the course of their inquiry they analyzed and x-rayed and dissected their victims. Some of the investigators were successful in their search and discovered solid evidence. Other authors were left with unfortified theories, vain surmises and sheer guesswork. The successful biographers revealed the springs of conduct in their figures, and their findings threw light on the mechanism of universal human nature.

A school of writers in the early twentieth century portrayed great men and women with emphasis on their deficiencies. Thus depicted, these figures seemed to belong to the human family and not to a race set apart. If they did not always appear to possess the same virtues of ordinary persons, they did have the limitations and defects of such individuals. The latter were comforted to find that heroes had weaknesses and made mistakes. Seeing frailties in high places, they felt that their own shortcomings were condoned. Biography had once been a means of inspiration. It now became in addition a medium both to level and to raise. If the reader chose, he could indulge in the happy illusion that he was on an equal moral and spiritual plane with the notables, if not superior to them.

Biography also serves as an aid in understanding human achievement. This use of biography applies more directly to literature, painting and other arts, but it likewise has a bearing on other fields in which men and women have laid their careers. Such knowledge is not indispensable in this respect. It is quite possible to understand and appreciate a work in the arts without knowing the life of the artist—even without knowing his name. Biographical information, however, takes the appreciator nearer to the author or painter and helps to illuminate the product of his labor. A poem or a novel, a portrait or a landscape, is more richly suggestive of its values if one is acquainted with the personality behind the work and the conditions under which it was created. The more subjective the work is, the clearer will be its meaning if the reader or observer is equipped with that knowledge. Whitman's *Leaves of Grass,* the sea tales of Herman Melville, the portraits by Gilbert Stuart, the lithographs of George Bellows, the musical compositions of Edward MacDowell—the work of each of these men, and of numberless others in the same fields, reveals new overtones to the person who is familiar with his life.

In the same way, biography gives the reader a better knowledge of the political philosophy of Thomas Jefferson, the educational principles of Horace Mann, the democratic economies of Henry George, the social service of Jane Addams, the scientific discoveries of George Washington Carver, and the accomplishments of other men and women.

⌐Another use of biography is that it lights up the past. A book of life-literature offers an approach to the time in which its protagonist lived. A famous actor can not be separated from the drama in which he made his name. Men and women who are reckoned great have always played a part in the transactions of their age. Their generation—or at least a portion of it—is reflected in their ambitions, activities and fortunes. The course of their lives can not be completely cut off from the general current of contemporary happenings. In order to show the full significance of an individual and to picture him in true perspective, a biography not only relates its figure to the area of the period in which he moved and made his impress, it also illuminates that setting.

Lives of high political leaders, if the works are authoritative, have a strong historical value. Biographies of Washington, Lincoln and Wilson carry the reader through the momentous events of great administrations. A similar panorama on a smaller scale—to name only a few—unrolls in the lives of John Marshall (by Albert J. Beveridge), John C. Calhoun (by Margaret L. Coit), Albert J. Beveridge (by Claude G. Bowers), and Elihu Root (by Philip C. Jessup). In more restricted fields, segments of the national history appear in the narratives of Daniel Boone (by John Bakeless) and of John C. Frémont (by Allan Nevins); chapters in American literary history are linked with the careers of Whitman, Howells and Dreiser; the abolition movement is set forth in the biographies of Wendell Phillips and William Lloyd Garrison; "the heroic age in American medicine" is interwoven with the achievement of William Henry Welch (by Simon Flexner and James T. Flexner); the development of the symphony orchestra in the United States is traced with the life of Theodore Thomas (by Charles Edward Russell); the American theatre for a half century forms the background of the career of David Belasco (by William Winter).

Biography is not a substitute for history. The record of a great man may epitomize an age, and it may be indicative of the tastes and trends of the time. It may fairly picture in a small compass the political, economic, literary, religious or other aspect of a period. [Again, a biography may give the reader glimpses of an age in general. No single work of life-literature, however, embraces the whole of an era.] The broadest chronicle of the life-and-times type does not follow the full course of a generation. The most distinguished life of a president can not take the place of a comprehensive history of the nation during his administrations. The finest biography of an author or a reformer or a medical man does not acquaint the reader with all the men and events in the sphere of his activity. Neither does a group of biographies form the equivalent of the historical work which integrates the different aspects of an era and is written from a broad rather than an individualized viewpoint. Biography and history have their respective functions; they must be read together for the best understanding of the past.[1]

[1]For the relation of the two subjects see the chapter "Biography and History" in Allan Nevins, *The Gateway to History*.

Chapter III

SOURCES OF THE BASIC
BIOGRAPHIC PRINCIPLES

Emerson said that an institution is the lengthened shadow of a man. By the same token biography may be called the extended reflection of Plutarch. The metaphor, however, oversimplifies the development of a complex form. It would be nearer to the truth to adapt Carlyle's definition that history is the essence of innumerable biographies and say that biography is the essence of innumerable biographers. For the textures and features of the form have been spun and shaped by many craftsmen of varying influence and importance. It is the purpose of the present chapter to consider the primary biographers who belong in this category and the philosophical and technical principles which American biography derived from them.

II

The foundation of biography is found in Plutarch. Although life-accounts, notably those in the Old and New Testaments, were in existence years before he wrote, the

Greek philosopher, who lived in the first century of the Christian era, was the parent of the subject as it is practised today. In his lives of celebrated Grecians and Romans, Plutarch used certain methods which have affected the nature of biographical writing since the late sixteenth century, when his work was first translated into English. He was long "an example and stimulus to English biographers." Workers in the art have repeatedly saluted him as master and guide. American biographers of every generation have been in debt to him.

"Personality was Plutarch's quarry." In his biography of Alexander he said that he would give his "more particular attention to the marks and indications of the souls of men," and would "endeavor by these to portray their lives." His design, he said, was "not to write histories, but lives," and he would leave "more weighty matters and great battles to be treated by others."

Plutarch pointed out the significance of seemingly small things about a man. "The most glorious exploits do not always furnish us with the clearest discoveries of virtue or vice in men; sometimes a matter of less moment, an expression or a jest, informs us better of their characters and inclinations, than the most famous sieges, the greatest armaments, or the bloodiest battles whatsoever. Therefore as portrait-painters are more exact in the lines and features of the face, in which the character is seen, than in the other parts of the body," so he would use a similar method in writing his lives.

In another passage he quotes Xenophon to the same effect: "The sayings of great men in their familiar discourses, and amidst their wine, have somewhat in them which is worthy to be transmitted to posterity."

The aim thus stated belongs to the essence of pure biography, but Plutarch did not stop at that point. He was a moralist, and he made his biographies a means of ethical instruction. He wrote in his life of Pericles: "Moral good is a practical stimulus; it is no sooner seen, than it inspires an impulse to practice, and influences the mind and character not by a mere imitation which we look at, but by the statement of the fact creates a moral purpose which we form."

Plutarch's lives were not extensive narratives. They were in the nature of sketches and essays, but they contained much history of the times in which his heroes lived. These men were warriors and statesmen, and the biographer followed them in the midst of happenings in which their characters were revealed. The comprehensive narrative, written wholly in the chronological order, was a later development in biography.

Plutarch used a method of portraying men by the synthesis of myriad bits of evidence. This is a fundamental principle of modern life-writing. He demonstrated the cumulative effect of concrete details and the construction of dramatic situations. He showed the value of anecdotes and directly quoted remarks. The ethical purpose which he employed was long a leading motive in biography.

Although Plutarch's lives contained praise of his subjects, the eulogistic strain came into American biography more strongly by another channel. From the earliest days of written memorials, the commemorative instinct had been accompanied by the desire to extol. Noble characters and glorious deeds deserved high words, and the ancient biographers praised their figures in lofty terms. The church fathers of the Middle Ages wrote from the same twofold purpose. In addition, they were inspired by the Gospels of the New Testament, and they made their chronicles of the saints strongly moralistic as well as panegyric. "The power of a life — the life of Jesus Christ — had entered into the world, and Christians, especially Churchmen, whose professional duty it was to point the way, were attempting to mould their lives after the Great Model."[1]

III

In the history of biographical criticism, so far as biography written in English is concerned, John Dryden is the chief figure between Plutarch and Samuel Johnson. Dryden made an important contribution to critical literature in connection with the translation of Plutarch's *Lives* which bears his name but was actually done by others. This was published in 1683. Dryden contributed to the work an account of Plutarch and also discussed the nature of biographical writing. He used the word *biography* for the first time and defined the form as "the history of particular men's lives." Dryden, however, thought of biography as one division of the broad field of history. In contrasting the writing of lives with the other two divisions, annals and history proper, he said that in biography:

"There is withal a descent into minute circumstances, and trivial passages of life, which are natural to this way of writing, and which the dignity of the other two will not admit. There you are conducted only into the rooms of state, here you are led into the private lodgings of the hero; you see him in his undress, and are made familiar with his most private actions and conversations . . . The pageantry of life is taken away: you see the poor reasonable animal as naked as ever nature made him; are made acquainted with his passions and his follies, and find the demi-god a man."

[1]Dunn, *English Biography,* p. 240.

Dryden also referred to Plutarch's practice of portraying men by "relating little passages," and he quoted the words which Plutarch had written in explanation of his method.

Dryden applied his own principles to his account of Plutarch, but neither this essay nor any other life by him became a model for later authors. Dryden's place in biographical history rests on his criticism rather than on example. Dryden gave a developing form of literature a name and a definition. He stated "the broad general principles" toward which earlier English biographers had been vaguely working, and he pointed the way to the purpose and plan of the future.

IV

Next to Plutarch, the joint shadows of Samuel Johnson and James Boswell—if Emerson's metaphor of an institution and a man may be pluralized—fall most influentially across the later course of biographical writing. The chapter of Johnson and Boswell is the salient feature of English biography in the latter part of the eighteenth century. The critical dicta made by Johnson and the concrete example furnished by his disciple were vital factors in the development of biography.

Johnson made the writing of lives a separate and distinct branch of literature, and gave the subject the status of an art. He expressed himself freely on its functions and methods, and laid down principles which passed into the general theory of the art. He valued biography "as giving us what comes near to ourselves, what we can turn to use." He declared for the kind of biography which was candid and truthful and free from cant and eulogy. "There are many," he said, "who think it an act of piety to hide the faults or failings of their friends, even when they can no

longer suffer by their detection. We therefore see whole
ranks of characters adorned with uniform panegyric, and
not be known from one another but by extrinsic and casual
circumstances."

Johnson complained of the unskilled and negligent writers who "imagine themselves writing a life when they exhibit a chronological series of actions or preferments; and
have so little regard to the manners or behavior of their
heroes, that more knowledge may be gained of a man's real
character, by a short conversation with one of his servants,
than from a formal and studied narrative, begun with his
pedigree, and ended with his funeral." Johnson opposed
the use of "striking or wonderful vicissitudes" simply for
their effect. He stated the same principle as Plutarch concerning the importance of small things in the delineation of
character: "The business of the biographer is often to pass
slightly over those performances and incidents which produce vulgar greatness, to lead the thoughts into domestic
privacies, and display the minute details of daily life, where
exterior appendages are cast aside, and men excel each
other only by prudence and by virtue." The great object
of Johnson's interest was human nature as it appeared in
the single individual. When put in biography, the individual should be drawn with "certainty of knowledge," psychologic insight, vivid detail and the full truth.[2]

V

When Boswell wrote his life of Johnson (1791), he applied the theory that the master had set down. Boswell
knew that the critical opinions of his friend formed the
best possible creed, and he knew that if he carried out the

---

[2] Johnson's criticism of biography appeared in the *Rambler,* No. 60, October
13, 1750; and the *Idler,* No. 84, November 24, 1759.

principles to the letter, he would faithfully serve his hero and his art. The work strikingly illustrates the effectiveness of Johnson's theory in the hands of a great artist.

The biography is noteworthy for the method by which it was composed. Boswell adopted a formula which brought Johnson directly to the pages of the book and made him an active participant in the unfolding of the narrative. Boswell said that he would not melt his materials into one mass and speak constantly in his own person. He would use another plan. "Wherever narrative is necessary to explain, connect, and supply," he continued, "I furnish it to the best of my abilities; but in the chronological series of Johnson's life, which I trace as distinctly as I can, year by year, I produce, wherever it is in my power, his own minutes, letters, or conversation, being convinced that this method is more lively, and will make my readers better acquainted with him." Boswell added that he could not "conceive a more perfect method of writing any man's life, than not only relating all the most important events of it in their order, but interweaving what he privately wrote, and said, and thought."

Boswell also declared that he would write not Johnson's panegyric but his Life. "In every picture there should be shade as well as light, and when I delineate him without reserve, I do what he himself recommended, both by his precept and his example."

Boswell supported this exposition of his method with documentation from two authorities. He cited Plutarch's statement regarding the significance of small things in the delineation of character, and he quoted at length Johnson's dicta on the writing of biography.

His plan, as Boswell told his readers, had originally been used in a smaller way by the Rev. William Mason in his

Memoirs of Thomas Gray (1775). Mason had made a real innovation in biography. He introduced Gray's letters in his work, but he did not insert them "merely as a part of the narrative; he used them to tell the story of Gray's life: in other words, he attempted to make Gray his own biographer."[3]

Mason seriously impaired his work, however, by altering the letters as he saw fit. Boswell enlarged upon Mason's plan by including passages from Johnson's writings and his utterances and conversations. Boswell also improved upon Mason's method and used it with far more honesty and skill. Johnson's career had been rich in anecdotes, and Boswell made liberal use of these stories.

The separate elements of Boswell's formula—the letters, the anecdotes and the conversation—had appeared before in English life-literature. He drew them together, along with the example established by Plutarch and the principles laid down by Johnson, to make a new method, and he applied the method to write a great biography.

VI

The *Life of Johnson* was published in 1791. An excellent model was thus available to American biographers of the early nineteenth century, but they did not adopt Boswell's work as a pattern. The effect of some literary models is immediate and clear. The early influence in America of Richardson in the novel, of Wordsworth in poetry and of Goldsmith in the essay is readily apparent. The impress of Boswell in biography can not be traced as easily, for his influence was more gradual and less perceptible. Some of the elements of Boswell's formula—the anecdote and ex-

---

[3]Dunn, *English Biography,* p. 108.

tracts from the talk and writings of biographical figures—
had previously appeared in American life-writing, although
no one had attempted to use the ingredients together as
Boswell did. The increasing frequency with which they
were employed in the Boswellian manner during the nineteenth century was undoubtedly caused in a large degree by
Boswell's example.

Neither did the early American authors accept Johnson's principle that biography should avoid the panegyric.
Instead they preferred to praise their figures and say only
good of them. Instinct and tradition were too strong for
the pronouncement of the critic. When the custom of
eulogy began to disappear, toward the close of the nineteenth century, the contributing factors came from other
sources rather than from Johnson's creed. His critical opinions, on the whole, seem to have confirmed the aims and
methods of later biographers rather than to have caused
them. It took the practice of biography in the United
States a long time to catch up with the sound judgment of
Dr. Johnson.

The basic principles from which American biography
developed were inherited from Plutarch, from the Gospel
narratives, from Dryden, and from Johnson and Boswell. In
the latter part of the nineteenth century and the first half
of the twentieth these principles were subjected to the play
of forces which amended and enlarged their function. The
nature of the forces will be considered in the section of this
volume in which the historical development of American
biography is traced.

CHAPTER IV

THE BIOGRAPHER AT WORK

A biography that satisfies the demands of its art brings an individuality to life clearly, truthfully and completely. In his endeavor to attain this end, the biographer is both compiler and creator. He is scientist as well as artist. He becomes witness and interpreter. Not infrequently he assumes the role of judge and critic. His work, stated in its simplest terms, embraces five parts. He collects his material, selects the essential and vital data, and converts that data in the correct proportion to make a unified whole. He supplements the business of portrayal by giving interpretation to his facts. Finally, he presents his conception of his figure in an adequate if not distinctive style. Each biographer handles the mechanics of his craft in his own way, and he adapts them to fit the man or woman whose life and character he is reconstructing. No two authors treat the same figure in identical fashion.

An art whose function is to re-create the characters and acts of real persons imposes a heavy responsibility on those who practise it. The responsibility carries a twofold moral and artistic duty. Biographers as a rule observe this obligation to their subjects, but the exceptions to the rule are too numerous for the good of the art. The character and career of every man and woman, living or dead, are in the public domain. Any individual may become the willing or involuntary hero or victim of any writer, qualified or not, who feels the impulse to biography. Many authors ask permission of their subjects or the immediate heirs, but this sanction is not legally necessary. A living person has no redress unless the biographer tells demonstrable falsehoods about him or goes to the extremes of libel or slander. He is likewise powerless in the case of the well-meant document which kills him with its kind extravagances or tortures him with its poor workmanship.[1]

Biography has profited from the true portraits drawn by its well-equipped workers. It has suffered from the deficiencies of the unskilled, the uncritical and the irresponsible. The superior facsimiles have preserved personalities and lives in an authentic and artistic manner; they have delighted and enlightened and inspired their readers without failing their subjects. Incompetent and erroneous volumes have not only done harm in their own time, but they have perpetuated their wrongs in the books of later authors. A work that is faithful to its figure does not invariably have

---

[1] In 1947 Serge Koussevitzky, conductor of the Boston Symphony Orchestra, took legal steps in New York City to prevent publication and distribution of a biography of himseslf by Moses Smith, a music critic of Boston. Dr. Koussevitzky claimsd that his right of privacy had been invaded. A justice of the Supreme Court in New York said in part in his decision that "the right of privacy statute does not apply to an unauthorized biography of a public figure unless the biography is fiction or novelized in character. An examination of the work clearly shows that it is not fictional."

The defense attorney argued that "biographies have always been a part of a free press" and that "if Dr. Koussevitzky should prevail here, every other public figure will be able to preclude the public from any facts about himself he chooses to withhold from scrutiny."

The decision of the justice was later upheld unanimously by the Appellate Division.

wide reading or permanent acceptance. Neither does a poor work always disappear under the weight of its shortcomings. Other factors—notably the appeal of the subject, the author's style and the entertainment value of the book—affect the fortunes of a biography.

A novel or a play that falls short of its art is instantly seen in its actual light. A work of biography can not always speak for itself. It must be judged for its validity by comparison with the original life. Relatively few laymen possess sufficient knowledge to make this measurement. They must rely on the honesty and the talents of the author.

"The reading of biography is for the layman—like his choice of a physician—an act of faith. In the latter instance he is able at least to evaluate to a degree the wisdom of his confidence by the state of his own health. But in biography there are only too many instances of the unsuspecting reading public accepting *in toto* a completely erroneous picture of the life and works of famous men."[2]

By the nature of his undertaking the biographer is charged with an obligation which is not assumed by the novelist and the dramatist. Unless they draw on history, the latter writers are free to create and treat their characters as they see fit. They are answerable only to themselves and to the canons of their arts. The worker in biography finds before him a character already developed and a life already lived. He is restricted to the actuality of a personal history. It is his high duty to record that history in faithful conformity to the original. He must match his powers with the challenge that is presented by his figure.

---

[2]From a review by William Schuman of *The Life and Works of Beethoven* by John N. Burk. The critic praises this biography and does not put the volume in the class to which he refers. *The New York Times Book Review*, June 27, 1943, p. 4.

II

The biographer must be equipped with certain qualities in order to meet this challenge. He must bring to his task an industry and patience in research. He should have a knowledge of human nature that will aid him to appraise men and events in general and his hero in particular. He should be informed on the background of the time in which the figure's career was laid. He must possess a keen insight and an acute perception that will lead to a thorough understanding of his protagonist, and a broad tolerance which, for the work in preparation, accepts his figure as the man was.

The practice of the biographer includes other requisites: a sense of discrimination that enables him to select the relevant and essential material from the accumulated product of his research; an imagination that vivifies but does not invent; a creative ability to unfold a smoothly flowing narrative and develop a rounded portrait; and the faculty of interpretation that explains and clarifies his hero. Furthermore, the author must infuse his biography with a vitality that lifts it from the level of a dry record to the status of living re-creation. With all these qualities the biographer should have an integrity which keeps faith with his art and strives for justice to the subject of his portrayal. These qualities constitute a large demand. They are found in their highest state in the biographer who is a genuine scholar and a true literary artist.

In his attitude toward his figure, the biographer as a rule feels an interest that is at least sympathetic, if not admiring or enthusiastic. He may be an ardent hero-worshipper and still maintain a judicial mind. He need not necessarily sanction the acts of his subject or subscribe to the latter's opinions or philosophy. Yet his pen is strengthened when the affinity exists, and the stronger the relationship, the more effective is the biography likely to be. It is possible for an author to write successfully of a man whom he dislikes. He may put aside his aversion and be fair to his figure. Undoubtedly a sound biography may be produced in an adverse frame of mind, but a constant antagonism to the figure is liable to impair the fidelity of the work. On the other hand, a strictly impersonal attitude tends to lessen the vividness of the portrait. The biographer who feels a temperamental harmony with his hero has, in this quality of "sympathy," a prime asset in understanding the man. The greatest biographies have been written from love.

III

The biographer finds his material in endless sources. Among these are the diary or journal kept by the person who is being studied, letters he wrote and received, his speeches and other utterances both public and private, and perhaps a fragmentary or a full autobiography. If the person was a writer, his works are read for their bearing on his life. Other sources are genealogies and family papers, oral information and reminiscent accounts given by individuals, official records of various kinds, especially the proceedings of legislative bodies, societies and other organizations, and contemporary newspapers and magazines.

Productive as all these sources may be, the biographer does not confine his interest to them. He may have the use of first-hand material already collected by another investigator. His figure may appear by mention or otherwise in numerous books as well as in the diaries, letters and autobiographies of other persons. Previous biographies of the same subject may be helpful, not only in furnishing the author with ideas and material, but also in showing him what to avoid in his biography. There is also scattered miscellaneous matter to be sought and examined, such as records of births and deaths, city directories, library catalogues, programs of theatrical performances and other events, passenger lists of ships, and photographs. Throughout his search the biographer must be constantly watchful for relevant information and for fresh clues that may lead to useful discoveries.[3]

The author strengthens his biography and heightens its atmosphere by having visited the scenes of the life he is transcribing and seeing at close hand the places where the figure lived and made his career. These places often yield valuable material. They also communicate graphic impressions which the biographer transmits to his pages.

In describing the preparation of her book, *John Adams and the American Revolution*, Catherine Drinker Bowen wrote:

"For the physical scene I found it necessary to visit Braintree in all four seasons. In the small tidy farmhouse where John was born, I went up narrow stairs, looked out a boy's dormer window onto February snow. I walked by Black's Creek when November held the salt grass stiff. John's great-great-granddaughter walked with me to show how she too had gone smelting in childhood between those marshy banks. I climbed Penns Hill in June as Abigail Adams had climbed it to see the Battle of Bunker Hill across the Bay.

---

[3]"The first thing to be done by a biographer in estimating character is to examine the stubs of his victim's cheque-books."—Quoted from Dr. S. Weir Mitchell by Harvey Cushing in his *Life of Sir William Osler*.

Some biographers employ assistants to aid them in the research and collection of material. The adventures of the authors and the helpers rarely appear in the pages of the biographies. Their experiences in this phase of the work would often make interesting if not exciting tales.

In Boston, the old State House still stands, and in Philadelphia, Independence Hall. All the bustle of the twentieth century cannot efface the spirits that walk within these walls."[4]

The wise biographer does not keep too closely to one source or authority unless that source is thoroughly unimpeachable. Few sources of extensive information possess the ideal quality of complete infallibility. With their soundness granted, numerous sources offer the advantage of different viewpoints and varied testimony.

The path of the investigator rarely runs smooth. He encounters many problems and difficulties in gathering his material. Witnesses, living or dead, furnish conflicting testimony on the same point. Persons who knew a great man give information of varied value. There are, to be sure, many individuals who are reliable in their evidence. Others are hazy, reticent or over-imaginative in their recollections, or they may, consciously or not, color their testimony to reflect the man's fame, to hurt his reputation or to gain attention for themselves.

Records may be silent or missing when they are needed most. "Facts" contradict one another, and their validity is determined only after long comparison with corroborative or opposing statements. The biographer must also be vigilant to detect garbled or false matter. Questions which arise in his mind require extensive research for answer and may never be solved decisively. Who is to be believed in a debatable instance—the figure or his enemy? Why does the evidence at one juncture in a man's life point to a conclusion that is palpably wrong? How much of a certain diary was colored with an eye for posthumous publication? To

---

[4]"The Business of a Biographer" in *The Atlantic Monthly*, Vol. 187, p. 52, May 1951.

what extent was the writer of a series of letters influenced by the personality and opinions of the recipient?

Letters are of varied value as sources of biographical information. They must be considered in the light of the writer's purpose and temperament. There are different kinds of correspondence: personal and business, private and public, and the type which combines the characteristics of any of these kinds. A letter, for example, which is addressed by a political leader to a close friend and is prepared for immediate publication may have the tone of an informal private communication. Letters which are written solely for the eyes of the recipient often yield genuine revelations of character and provide useful data to the biographer. Yet as a generic source they are not an infallible medium. Men and women do not necessarily open their hearts in private correspondence, nor are they always truthful or accurate in personal letters. They may be candid, inhibited, indirect, self-deceptive. Rashness is not a sure token of veracity, nor does reserve on the part of the writer necessarily mean that he is withholding important matter.

Letters which the writer knows will possibly be published are apt to have a different value. Honest and informative as they may be, the writer composes them with the idea of publication in mind, and this contingency frequently shapes their contents. The compiler of a life considers the circumstances of all letters in weighing the merits of his subject's correspondence. He relates the letters to the immediate context of the man's activities. He studies the lines and reads between the lines. He tests the contents by other data.

IV

In previous paragraphs some of the problems which con-

front the biographer were discussed. The truth which remains hidden in material of this kind is determined in various ways: by comparison of authorities, by circumstantial
evidence, by direct inference or reasoning, or by that intuition that is sure though it can not demonstrate its conclusions. In arriving at his decisions, the biographer must
often depend on his own judgment, supported as far as possible by the data which bears upon the puzzle before him.
Even when obstacles of this kind are few or are wholly in-
existent, the conscientious biographer has no small labor
in the ordinary routine of reading and research. In any
case, he must combine the qualities of a patient investigator, a skilled detective and a wise judge.

His task becomes more intricate as he weighs his material
and selects the portions he is to use. From the beginning
of his research until his work is finished, it may be said that
the biographer lives the life of his subject. At this point in
his undertaking that vicarious method is intensified, as he
analyzes and studies the figure with deliberation, observant
of outer actions and alive to the revelations of individuality.
What qualities and acts should be chosen as typical of the
man? What of the things that are contrary to his general
nature? To present the exceptional as representative is as
misleading as to make the habitual appear uncommon. Rus-
kin said that to know a man rightly we must know him
completely. Yet the problem of portraying the "whole" man
adequately is not solved merely by including the faults in
his character or the ignoble acts in his conduct. The use of
these things contributes to the totality of the presentment,
but it can not always be said of biographers that if they
know the truth, the truth will make them artists. All the
man's characteristics and acts must be used in the correct
proportion, with due regard to the typical and the excep-

tional. In some cases it is difficult for the investigator to determine the true ratio of the virtues and vices of his figure. The testimony may be unanimous that the man possessed a mixture of opposing qualities, but there is strong disagreement among the witnesses as to the apportionment of these credits and debits in his character. Edgar Allan Poe is a figure who has been an object of dissent in this respect.

The biographer also seeks to understand motives, and he notes reactions. Is it possible to establish a man's motives beyond question, and how shall that be done? What do the marks of personality actually disclose? The diagnosis of character imposes problems of this kind on the author. The difficulty in answering them has been summed up by Gamaliel Bradford, a biographer of long experience: "The most minute study, the widest experience in the investigation of human actions and their motives, only make us feel more and more the shifting, terrible uncertainty of the ground under our feet." Although he retains his position as the student of a life—firm, patient and unyielding—the biographer projects himself into the career of his subject, frequently taking the other's point of view, and seeing, feeling and acting with him. In this way the dead and ended past of a person's life becomes for the biographer the living and unfolding present.

V

To include everything of the original life is neither feasible nor desirable. A biography which attempted to achieve this range would run to interminable length and would defeat its purpose by its magnitude. The term "complete life" means that the biography in question extends from birth to death and contains the essential facts in sufficient detail. "The art of the biographer should enable him to make a selection of materials which in artistic combination shall produce an effect most nearly similar to what the whole mass of incidents would produce, if it were possible for them to be minutely represented."[5]

Waldo H. Dunn, a historian of English biography, refers to a defect in biographical writing which Herbert Spencer had pointed out. " 'A biographer or autobiographer is obliged to omit from his narrative the commonplaces of daily life, and to limit himself almost exclusively to salient events, action, and traits. The writing and the reading of the bulky volumes otherwise required would be alike impossible. But by leaving out the humdrum part of life, forming that immensely larger part which it had in common with other lives, and by setting forth only the striking things, he produces the impression that it differed from other lives more than it really did. The defect is inevitable.' " Dr. Dunn grants the necessity of these omissions in great degree and adds that the defect "is less noticeable in the works of those biographers who possess the highest artistic ability."[6]

There is no uniform standard which tells the author what to select and what to leave. The ingredients of each life must be examined and appraised, not only in themselves, but in their relation to one another and to the entire life.

The material selected is made up of an infinite quantity of parts which differ widely in substance, length and importance. The nature of the parts and their relation to one another have a special significance to the author when he arranges them for his narrative. Here he is concerned with the proportion and emphasis the larger parts should have. What is the importance of each? How much space does

---

[5] "Biography," *Southern Literary Messenger*, Vol. 23, p. 282, October 1856.

[6] *English Biography*. p. 225.

each require for proper elucidation? These are the chief questions to be decided. The structure of the whole biography must also be laid out. The scale to which the original life is reduced depends upon the prospective length of the narrative, whether the biographer plans a work of a single volume or of two or more volumes.

The first draft of the manuscript is followed by one or more revisions. This chapter and that may be rewritten several times, perhaps many times, before they are in a state which satisfies the biographer. Certain portions of the narrative may be condensed, and others expanded. Some passages may be taken out, and new parts inserted. Dates, references and other details are checked for their accuracy. Some chapters and perhaps the whole manuscript are sent to authorities and specialists for their critical opinions. The original manuscript undergoes changes of one kind or another, and it is continually polished in statement and style before the author can feel that the biography is, relatively speaking, finished. Even then the exact degree of the feeling of completeness depends on the temperament of the biographer.

VI

The structure of a biography is governed by the purpose of the author and his arrangement of his material. The method commonly used is the chronological order. This is the natural plan for a biographer to follow in presenting the continuity of happenings and successive changes in the life of his figure. A narrative of this kind may be long and detailed or short and condensed. By another method the writer ignores the time-sequence and depicts his subject in one long essay, or in a series of essays which, taken together, are intended to make a rounded portrait. The latter plan was used by Paul Leicester Ford in *The True George Washington* (1896), by William I. Hull in his topical biography of William Penn (1937), and by Will D. Howe in *Charles Lamb and His Friends* (1944). The chronological and the essay-group methods furnish the basic framework of biographical writing. They are employed separately or together in varied arrangements. Gamaliel Bradford used the combined essay and time-order methods in *Lee the American* (1912).

Another procedure is open to biographers. The interest of many persons is often drawn to a man for the first time by a notable achievement or event in his life. This may be a discovery or an invention, a work in one of the arts, a phase of a political or military career, or a remarkable experience. A biography might well begin with an account of that particular thing. The author would then go on to other related accomplishments and happenings, and afterward turn to the earlier and later parts of the individual's life. This is the way in which some readers go about to obtain knowledge of a man, and a biography written in this manner would only follow the natural course of their interest.

Three narrative biographies which do not follow the usual time-order of events are *Hanna* (1929) by Thomas Beer, *A Man Named Grant* (1940) by Helen Todd, and *Thomas: Rock of Chickamauga* (1948) by Richard O'Connor. *Hanna* opens in 1865 with the assassination of Lincoln, twenty-eight years after the birth of its figure. The first chapter of the biography of Grant shows him seeking an interview with General McClellan in 1861. The chronicle of Thomas begins at Chickamauga Creek, where "Old Pop" made a heroic stand.

Chapter V

INTERPRETATION

The guiding principle of the biographic process is exposition. The principle runs through the greater part of the author's undertaking. It governs his selection of material. It continues in larger degree as he adapts and molds the material, amplifies and develops the parts, inserts the connecting links, and carries the chronicle through to the end.

Biographies in general are compounds of three things. The basic data concerning the hero and his life is the backbone of the work. This is supplemented by matter of various kinds which is needed to round out the reader's knowledge. The additional parts consist of outlines of family pedigrees, descriptions of the backgrounds of city or country where the man lived from childhood to old age, sketches of the friends and associates who were connected with his life, mention of incidental persons and happenings, and explanations of issues and philosophies that affected his career. All this and similar matter must be filled in and blended with the basic data to satisfy the demands of clearness and completeness. The supplemental information varies in amount according to the author's purpose and treatment. The biographer may restrict that part of his work to the bare essentials, or he may extend it at length.

The third part of the biography is the interpretative element. This is the actuating principle of the work. It is a more intricate and subtle form of the explanatory process. Interpretation is obtained from the data the biographer selects, the meaning he attributes to it, and the diction and phraseology he uses in expressing the meaning. Interpretation is further achieved by suggestion and implication, by the author's comments and opinions, and by quoted statements from other persons. Interpretation is the constituent which, in its genuine state, brings out the meaning and significance of the human beings and human affairs that are set forth in the work. It lights up traits of individuality, the acts of the central figure and his contemporaries, and the happenings in their lives. It translates literal statistics into expressive symbols. It quickens the reader's perception and heightens his understanding. It connotes overtones which lie in the portrait and narrative. It adds a new dimension to the chronicle.

The ideal of the interpretative principle is to present the elements of the data with the same meaning which they had in the personality and life of the subject. Facts in themselves are not invariably self-sufficient. They have origins and effects, and implications and relationships, which require explanation. They need to be sifted and put in order, analyzed and illumined. It is not hard for an author to attribute meanings of some kind to the fruit of his research. The great difficulty is to recover the exact sense which the facts had in their original state, when the figure lived and acted them. Insofar as the biographer accomplishes this in his work, his facsimile agrees with the original in spirit as well as in letter. His biography has a truth which transcends the facts.

What *is* the right letter of the record? What *is* the exact sense of the facts? What just deductions can be drawn from the data? What, in short, is the true man? These questions make the practice of biography an endless quest. Behind the search for the answers are the complex individualities of the subjects and the personal equations of the biographers.

In studying a biographical figure, an author must consider the numerous viewpoints from which the man was seen during his lifetime. First there is the attitude of the protagonist toward himself. How much acceptance should the biographer give to the hero's judgment and estimate of his own traits and acts? How much weight should the man's equation have in the process of interpretation? Besides the autobiographical viewpoint, the author meets various other attitudes during his research. In his relationships in life, a man appears in different lights to different persons. He is one thing to his mother, another to his wife, a third to his physician, and he is observed in still other guises by his friends and others. Despite these varied concepts, he is a man of a single individuality, although he may show different sides of his nature to those persons. Moreover, they see him under different circumstances. Behind the separate points of view are the personal equations of the observers and their reactions to his individuality. A detached biographer considers the viewpoints of family, friends and others toward his subject. He tries to discover the real individuality uncolored by any emotional or intellectual bias. Yet in the end his interpretation of his hero is governed by his own equation.[1]

----

[1] Some biographers who have been closely associated with their figures treat the subjects with special emphasis on their own point of view. Examples are *Life of Alice Freeman Palmer* (1908) by George Herbert Palmer, *My Mark Twain* (1910) by William Dean Howells, and *The Roosevelt I Knew* (1946) by Frances Perkins.

Whatever preconceived ideas of his hero the author may have, he should let his portrayal grow from scratch out of the material he assembles, or he should alter his opinions, if that is necessary, to conform to the evidence. Conversely, the author should guard against the posthumous influence of a figure whom he cherishes or venerates. Magnetic personalities have the power to charm the biographer. They may induce him to defend the indefensible, to make unwarranted apologies in their favor, or to soften their mistakes. Biographers have human susceptibilities as well as their heroes.

The *personal equation* "signifies the moral, mental and temperamental qualities and idiosyncracies" of the author. The mechanism of the equation guides interpretation and shapes decisions. It is the still voice that is always at his ear and the moving finger that directs his pen. It fashions the author's style. In judging a biography, a critical reader takes into consideration the personal qualities, the point of view and the particular philosophy of the author. Two personalities—each with its own set of human traits—go into the making of every biography. The resulting work shows the effect of the biographer upon his subject and the effect of the subject upon the interpreter.

II

Complex as the process of biographical interpretation is, two general methods appear in the practice. Each method has its variations and nuances. Each blends into the other at times. No attempt is made here to shape these methods into fixed patterns, but the distinguishing features of the two lines of procedure may be examined.

Interpretation is objective and subjective. In the former the burden of truth and proof lies with the figure who is being studied. He is called upon to explain himself by the autobiographical method. In the latter use of the principle the burden falls on the biographer. Interpretation in the subjective sense belongs to the theoretics of biography. To the writer who is a skeptic this form of interpretation is speculative. To the cynic it is guesswork. The impostor knows the imagined motives and the invented thoughts he has inflicted on his subject and foisted on the public. The realist is conscious of the perplexities and uncertainties which confront the biographer, the puzzles which can never be solved, and the elation which follows the positive solution of a vexatious problem.

When applied in the objective form, interpretation achieves its purpose by the use of firsthand data almost exclusively. A biography written in this manner has little or no critical opinion from the author. It does not contain in concrete terms his reactions to the elements of his data. He neither defends nor condemns, he does not applaud or disparage. He reconstructs the character and career of his hero by weaving together the pertinent data which have been yielded by documented sources. The author employs the autobiographical method at times, quoting directly from the man's diary, letters or papers, his conversations and public utterances, and allowing the figure to speak for himself and explain his ideas and acts. The objective biographer is a detached reporter of a life, although the detachment implies no lack of sympathy, insight or vividness in his work.

No matter how rich and voluminous the records are, the findings of the biographer can not be arranged in a coherent and complete whole without the addition of original passages. There are always things which the figure does not say about himself and the setting of his life. Wherever it is necessary, the author must supply explanatory remarks and descriptive sidelights, and he must fill in the gaps which occur in the course of his narrative. Even though he maintains an objective attitude, no biography can be completely objective in its contents. The human equation is always at work. The preferences or the enthusiasms of a re-creative artist can hardly be wholly excluded from the pages of a long chronicle.

When the objective method is used, the play of the author's subjective faculty is not visible to the reader. Yet the faculty works actively off the pages in selecting material and weighing evidence. There are often moot points to be decided, and differing versions of a problematic topic to be sifted. Biographers of Lincoln, for example, formerly found conflicting testimony regarding his religion and his friendship with Ann Rutledge. They either discussed the debatable evidence before the reader or made their decisions privately without acquainting him with the questions involved. The subjective faculty operates throughout the author's whole undertaking in his attempt to obtain a clear and unbiassed conception of his figure and to make the likeness intelligible to the reader. The principle of interpretation does not require that the biographer adopt the role of advocate, teacher or magistrate, or that he put his technique on view. Neither does the principle demand that he always uncover motives. His duty is to make his figure understood. If he attains that end, he has interpreted the man.

III

Objective interpretation is exemplified in Henry Steele Commager's biography of Theodore Parker (1936), the Unitarian minister and reformer of Boston. Emerson considered Parker one of the three greatest men of the time;

Parker once called himself the best-hated man in America.
He and his contemporaries left an "embarrassingly voluminous" quantity of writings, letters and personal journals,
and recorded conversations. In the preface of his book Dr.
Commager explains the principle by which he wrote the life.
Although he disclaims having a theory of biography, his
exposition amounts to an analysis of the objective method
as it was applied to Theodore Parker. Dr. Commager says
in part:

"Nor have I been interested in passing judgment on
Parker or in stating the verdict of history upon the movements in which he so energetically participated. I have
tried to present Parker and his contemporaries as they appeared to themselves and to each other, rather than as they
appear to a generation wiser, perhaps, certainly more sophis-
ticated and more disillusioned.

". . . It is Parker's life, not my own reactions to it,
that I have tried to tell: his interests, opinions, emotions,
prejudices if you will, that I have tried to interpret . . . I
have been anxious in writing this book to get at the essence
of Parker's character and thought and to explain it. I have
tried to know and to feel what Parker and his friends knew
and felt, to accept the limitations of their minds and, perhaps, of their characters. I have tried to see men and measures with Parker's eyes, to react to the events of the time
as he did, or as I think he did. I have permitted Parker
to act as he chose to act, to render such judgment as he
wished to make, to love those friends whom he did love,
and to disparage those persons whom he disliked, whether
he was wise in all this, or unwise. Where he was vain I
have not sought to rebuke his vanity, where he was inconsistent I have not thought it necessary to remark his incon-
sistency, where he was ungenerous I have not taken him to

task, where he was violent I have not tried to abate his vio-
lence, where he was mistaken I have not attempted to set
him right: all these things he confessed in his own words and
actions and they appear without my intervention. It would
be easy enough, and dangerous, too, to say, Here history has
proved him right, here wrong, here his judgment has been
vindicated, here impeached. It is better that the reader
should have the satisfaction of doing this for himself . . ."

In the final chapter of the book Dr. Commager supplements the method by making his own analysis of Parker's
character and mind. This analysis, it should be noted, describes Parker in terms of his actual proven qualities. Clear,
rounded and just, the summary is an admirable conclusion to the life.

Another notable biography that illustrates the objective
method is *Benjamin Franklin* (1938) by Carl Van Doren.
"In effect," the author says, "Franklin's autobiography is
here completed on his own scale and in his own words."
In his memoirs Franklin did not record the last thirty years
of his life. That was the climactic period of his career,
during which "he developed from a competent provincial
into an able, cultivated, and imposing man of the world."
Franklin left abundant material concerning those years, scattered through his writings, and thus his unfinished history
of himself may be completed from his own sources. Mr.
Van Doren lets Franklin tell his own story and draw his own
portrait, as far as that is possible, but the biographer must
necessarily supply an enormous amount of explanatory matter and connecting parts in order to maintain the continuity.
In these passages he makes his own style harmonize with
the clear, effortless style of his subject. Franklin has always
been his best interpreter—he stamped almost everything he
wrote with the marks of his personality—but skillful crafts-

manship was required to fashion his data into a proportioned, unified, full-length biography.

The tenor of the book, which runs to eight hundred pages, is shown by a statement the author makes in the concluding paragraph: "He has here told his story, which ends with his life. Nor should there now be need of a further comment on the record. Let the record stand, and explain itself."

The life of Alexander Hamilton (1946) by Nathan Schachner is another example of a biography written in the objective manner. In the case of Hamilton the author is dealing with a figure of a complex nature, contradictory acts and a controversial political philosophy. Statesmen with records of this kind have often made advocates or prosecutors of their biographers, but Mr. Schachner neither defends nor impugns his subject. Without prejudice or partisanship he skillfully reconstructs the Hamiltonian chapter of American history. He applies the reasoning faculty in choosing his data and maintains a judicial attitude in the chronicle. The biography does justice to its hero as well as to Jefferson and the other characters in its pages. Rounded and complete, the biography is satisfying and convincing to the impartial reader who would see Hamilton and his contemporaries in their own age and watch momentous history being made. Mr. Schachner gives the reader nearly five hundred pages of evidence on which to base his judgments of the actors.

Every great man should be set forth in an objective biography. Irrespective of subjective portrayals and critical studies, there should be one book in which a figure of historic stature is allowed to re-enact his life without critical appraisal from the biographer and the conflicting judgments of later generations. Men who leave voluminous records of definite information about themselves are in an excellent position to benefit from this objectivity. Ralph Waldo Emerson is a man who belongs in the category. He is the subject of a biography (1949) by Ralph Leslie Rusk. The author's purpose, as it is stated in the preface, is to let Emerson "and his contemporaries speak for themselves and act as they did in real life without much regard to our preconceived notions of them." The principle of letting a man speak for himself is deceptively intricate and exacting. Besides the investigation of sources and the deliberation over usable data, the principle requires an understanding which unites the figure's self-knowledge and the insight of a judicious author. The demands of the method are fully met here in a distinguished biography which transcends dated volumes on Emerson and becomes permanent in its interest and value.

Biographies which interpret their figures objectively have been criticised on the ground that the authors bring nothing to their books that was not in the lives and records of the men. If historians and biographers refuse criticism and subjective interpretation to us in their works, the argument runs, where are we to turn for illumination and understanding of the past and the actors in it?

If all historians and biographers had written as accurately, clearly, acutely and fully as the authors just discussed, many of the actors in history and the characters in biography would be better understood than they are. The truth about their personalities and lives would not have become confused by a multiplicity of subjective interpretations frequently based on unproved hypotheses, splenetic bias and partisan formulas. Biography has a place for the verdicts of the authority, but the findings should be judicial. In competent objective works, the source of illumination and the means of understanding are available to readers who bring an open mind to the evidence and desire to form their own opinions. Furthermore, if all biographic figures had been fortunate enough to leave written records as voluminous and perspicuous as those of Franklin, Parker and Emerson, they would furnish their own materials of illumination and understanding. A host of historic personages have not been equally kind to their biographers.

IV

The biographer who uses the subjective method of presenting his protagonist begins his task with the same aim of the objective author. Like his fellow-craftsman he seeks to discover the essence of his hero's character. He tries to see and think and feel with his figure. He allows the man to show engaging or unlovely qualities, to reveal abilities or limitations, to rise in triumph or fall in failure. In short, if he is true to his art, the author grants the players in his drama full freedom to act as they did in real life.

From this point on the subjective biographer differs from the detached historian. He visibly associates himself with the life of his figure and expresses his personal reactions when and where he sees fit. This subjective matter varies widely in nature and scope. According to the circumstances, the author may ascribe causes, infer motives and draw conclusions. He may uphold or censure, pronounce innocence or guilt, and assert his figure's wisdom or folly. He may explain a social or an economic question, a political issue or military tactics and add his own opinions to the exposition. He may analyze a literary work or a musical composition and combine his critical views with the meaning of the author or composer. He may become the dramatist vocally present on the stage in the part of critic, moralist or philosopher. All this is not to say that the subjective biographer is captious, arbitrary or dogmatic, although these qualities exist in the craft.

The value of the critical and judicial matter depends on two things: the qualifications of the author to act in those capacities and the nature of his pronouncements. A biography gains unquestionably by the judgments and convictions of an expert who has lived long with his hero. Comparatively few laymen have the knowledge that is needed to arrive at the verdicts of the specialist. Yet the question may be raised as to what the layman is to do when the authorities disagree. His solution is to study the biographic specialists—to become acquainted with all sides of a problematic topic—and to make up his own mind about it. The nature of the biographer's opinions also affects the worth of his work. When the subjective matter clarifies the data, when it becomes a catalytic medium between the figure and the reader, when it serves to appraise men and women on the basis of actual evidence, those portions of a biography perform a useful function. They often furnish the final degree of interpretation that consummates the reader's understanding.

Lives written by the subjective method are liable to certain faults that do not appear in objective works. These defects are not general to the class, but they are inevitable in the type of biography that is affected so largely by the author's equation. An immoderate laudatory strain through the narrative or a continual hostile tone toward the figure lessens the value of the biography to persons who are not partisans. These elements raise doubt in the reader's mind as to the faithfulness of the portrait. Eulogy and ill will are readily recognized. Less apparent to the ordinary reader are the ways in which a writer may color his material or use his data to aid or hurt his subject. Derogatory matter is minimized or played up; undue emphasis is put on a man's virtues or failings; to suit his purpose the author may give precedence in importance to favorable or unfavorable witnesses. A satirical attitude on the part of the author may be entertaining to some readers, yet this manner, which is an adulterant in biography, adds no truth to the chronicle and no accuracy to the portrait. A life is also weakened by conclusions that are not clearly supported by the evidence that is cited. A biography that is written to grind an axe may achieve its purpose, but it is open to distrust. It is seen that the defects of the subjective method that have been enumerated here originate in the biographer rather than in the figure or the material.

V

The objective and subjective methods of interpretation are different means to the same end. Any man or woman may be treated by both methods, although the resulting product will not be the same in each case, irrespective of the skill of the biographer. The objective process is the more restrictive of the two procedures. As the author excludes his explicit reactions from the account, he must depend more heavily on the source-material for the interpretation. If his figure was a man of speech and pen, the utterances and writings offer him authentic aid in composing the narrative. The richer and more extensive this autobiographical matter is, the further and deeper the biographer may go in his portrayal. A potential weakness of the objective method is that it will not bring out the spiritual and intangible as fully as the physical and external. If the subject's self-record reveals his inner life sufficiently, this contingency may be met successfully by the biographer. If the spiritual record is lacking, the author is at a disadvantage in this phase of his work. A final feature of this method is that it does not make up the reader's mind for him. If the author is truly objective, the reader is left to form his own judgments and conclusions.

The subjective method in its varying forms has been used far more numerously by American biographers. The obvious advantage of the method is that it gives the author greater scope in making his hero known. Before he reaches the stage of interpretation, the biographer has studied the man. He has absorbed the meaning and significance of his material and has pondered his findings. He may then, in the process of re-creation, invest the chronicle with the impressions, reflections and reactions that he has derived from his research and study. If he does not violate the basic data, he has freedom to construe his figure, to state his own judgments, to insert what seems necessary to make the data clear and complete. The use of the autobiographical method with the author's interpretation is notably effective.

The potentialities of the subjective method have been admirably demonstrated in the works of informed and sensitive biographers. A short illustrative list of such authors and their subjects (not necessarily the titles) follows.

Joseph Q. Adams. Shakespeare (1923)
William C. Bruce. Benjamin Franklin (1917)
Henry S. Canby. Thoreau (1939)
David Donald. William H. Herndon (1948)
Esther Forbes. Paul Revere (1942)
Douglas S. Freeman. R. E. Lee (1934, 1935)
Claude M. Fuess. Daniel Webster (1930)
Marquis James. Andrew Jackson (1933, 1937)
Allan Nevins. Grover Cleveland (1932)

Carl Sandburg. Lincoln (1926, 1939)
Odell Shepard. Amos Bronson Alcott (1937)
Nathaniel W. Stephenson. Lincoln (1922)
George F. Whicher. Emily Dickinson (1938)
George E. Woodberry. Edgar Allan Poe (1909)

Chapter VI

BIOGRAPHIC PROGRESSION
AND PORTRAYAL

The multiplication of books about the same heroes is a familiar phenomenon in biography. The practice of rewriting the lives of figures of the past has long been established. No matter how authentic or well written the chronicles of previous years may be, each succeeding age desires its own portraits and narratives. Such is the decree of custom. Biographers who offer new lives speak of the need in their forewords. Reviewers hail "fresh" interpretations. Responsive readers lay aside older biographies and pick up the latest volumes. There is always an air of promise about a new history of a classic figure—a promise which may be fulfilled or not. In many cases one biography of a famous person is not enough, adequate though it may be; the life of the same subject may be multiplied several times within a decade. The same process of repetition is continued without end. There is no planned economy in the realm of biography. The system of free enterprise rules, and authors choose their heroes at will. Despite errors and excesses and failures, the practice of rewriting lives has in the main pointed toward the goal of the ideal work. It may represent nature's attempt to produce a perfect biography.

In the course of human events certain men and women live on in their fame and influence. They become the historic property of posterity. By the work they did or by their effect on society they have a continuing significance in future times. Every generation has a logical interest in the nature of this significance and in the position of the immortals in its own time. The impress made by a man, together with its meaning, can not be separated from his character and acts; consequently the same interest embraces his personality and career as well. Out of all this varied curiosity each generation writes its own biographies and makes its own interpretations and evaluations in the light of its experience and perspective.

People do not cling to old biographies as they cherish classic novels and poems. Unless it possesses lasting qualities of portrayal and style, a biography suffers a handicap in proportion to its age. Comparatively few American biographies of the nineteenth century have competed successfully with later lives of their figures.[1]

The necessity of a new biography may be real or fancied. The actual need of a new life of a person who has already been portrayed arises for several reasons. Research workers and other persons discover source-material that has been lost or hitherto unknown. Families open their private papers to responsible authors and allow the use of diaries and letters which have previously been withheld. The family pa-

---

[1]Among these are *Life of Andrew Jackson* (1860) by James Parton, *Life of Thomas Paine* (1892) by Moncure D. Conway, and *The True George Washington* (1896) by Paul Leicester Ford. A great political biography of the last century, *Life of Albert Gallatin*, published in 1879, by Henry Adams, has never been superseded. When this note is made, no full-length biography of Gallatin has been published in the twentieth century.

pers and other things that are brought to light frequently yield information which corrects the features of former portraits. The new material may prove the truth or error of earlier data and enlarge the existing fund of knowledge of the figure. New lives are also needed if prior accounts of the subjects have been warped by eulogy or the malice of the authors. A new biography that contains fresh material of importance, or one that surpasses its predecessors in reproducing the letter and spirit of the original record, is amply justified, regardless of the transitory demands of the time.

Biographies continue to be written and read whether or not they contain fresh material or excel former lives of the same figure. The latest biographies are not always actually new, nor are they invariably the best chronicles of their subjects. They may be more or less rewritten versions brought seemingly up-to-date in treatment and style. Several factors, however, contribute to the possibility that the latest written biographies will be of the superior order. The authors have the use of new and old material, they profit from the merits and mistakes of their predecessors, and they gain by the use of improved technical principles. Excellent biographies, nevertheless, have been written of figures who have never been set forth at full length before.

Contemporary works satisfy the desire of an age for its own lives. Newness is the telling point in their favor. Newness in itself is, of course, no assurance of superior portraiture or an adequate presentation of a man's life. As a rule, new biographies conform to the trends and tastes of their time. They are written in styles that meet the favor of their immediate audience. They appraise achievements and determine failures according to current judgments. They present, as prospective readers anticipate, the latest interpretation of life histories and explain the present-day significance of their figures. Although recent generations have demanded general adherence to their own standards, they have not been averse to accepting a superior work which departed from the transient fashions.

II

It is plain that the limits of a life record are birth and death. The subsequent fate of a man's reputation and the verdict which posterity renders on him can not alter his character as it was or change his life as he lived it. Although the birth-to-death register is closed in its entries for all time, posterity supplements the record and makes its own entries in the biographies of future years. Each personal record is thus subjected to the multiple forces of later generations, and the individual who made the record faces fluctuating fortunes in the court of future opinion.

New biographies in any period presumably aim to answer two leading questions: What was the man in his time? What does he mean to us today? These questions involve the data of the subject's record and its interpretation. If the author makes his biography a critical study also, the book contains the element of appraisal. It evaluates the man's work and indicates his position, according to the critic's view, in his sphere of activity. The attempt to answer those two questions exposes the original record to certain hazards.

Like human beings, every generation has an equation. Prominent in it are the qualities that are peculiar to the age. Like the subjective biographer, the generation is governed by its temperament in construing figures of the past. The age-temperament shapes the course of the predominant opinions, but it can not enforce its ideas on the whole era. An age is rarely in complete agreement within itself about historical personages; almost invariably there are dissenting voices. Under all these circumstances a biographical character is subject to divergent interpretations in a single generation. As philosophies and ideals differ from one period to another, any figure who is treated in this manner becomes the recurring beneficiary or victim of the existing attitudes. The man and his career thus become enveloped in a welter of personal and period interpretations.

An author once said that a biographer must have regard to the interests and ethical standards of the generation for which he writes. Now the interests of any generation are broad and varied. They include prejudices as well as sympathies. Some interests are momentary; others are permanent. Some are the common attributes of the whole period; others belong only to a phase of the time. There are opposing and conflicting interests in every generation. Out of all these categories, which ones should the biographer choose as the legitimate objects of his regard? Which ones, if any, should he rightly consider in the portrayal and interpretation of his hero? If an author aims to synthesize his data in a clear and accurate presentation, there is no place in his chronicle for the interests of another generation. If he wishes to inform his readers of his reactions to his subject, the tastes and trends of his time should not alter his judgments. In "regarding" the interests as well as the ethical standards of his generation, the biographer not only exposes his hero to the influence of irrelevant factors, but he may also color his chronicle with the particular concerns and principles which he chooses to observe.

Appraisal is a legitimate function of a competent biographer—provided that he keeps that strand of his narrative fabric clear in the mind of the reader. A source of danger to a life record lies in the indiscriminate mixing of appraisal with interpretation. When this occurs, the evaluation of character and achievement is made from the standpoint of the period in which the biographer writes, but the result is treated as if the estimate were contemporaneous with the figure's career. The real function of interpretation, it may be repeated, is to explain the meaning, relationship and significance of facts. A generation should know before it judges. The interpretation belongs to the hero's period; the appraisal belongs to the age in which the biography is written. The two functions naturally coincide in those works which are prepared in the subject's lifetime or immediately after his death. When the factual testimony of one period is confused with the subjective judgments of a later time, the true character and acts of a man may be obscured or lost. The danger is lessened if interpretation and appraisal are kept separate before the reader.

The biographic art is served best by the work which not only re-creates the individuality and life of its hero solely from the materials of his own time, but also interprets him in the terms of that time. It shows the man as he saw himself and as he appeared to his contemporaries. These combined subjective and objective viewpoints point the way to the authentic portrait, which the biographer extracts from all the testimony. The witnesses observed him in different lights; they knew him in his private circle and in his public position; they may have magnified him, or they may have depreciated or misunderstood him. In determining the inner truth behind their external attitudes, the author considers the personal equations of the contemporary individuals.

The biographer recognizes the advantages that come from

contemporary knowledge and familiarity, as well as the drawbacks that lie in the lack of perspective. The passage of years and the human experience which accrues from time are powerful aids toward clarifying a biographical character. Yet time is a double-edged instrument of test. It is not an infallible guide to the measure of a man. If it dispels falsehoods and corrects errors, it also fosters myths and strengthens prejudices. In his attempt to obtain a clear vision, the biographer avoids these dangers of time and tempers the portrait he distills from contemporary evidence with all the benefits afforded by perspective. He takes care not to alter his figure's life by introducing factors from a later time, and he does not anticipate the opinions of the future.

CHAPTER VII

TYPES OF BIOGRAPHIC WRITING

Critics of biographies charge now and then that certain written lives are too short or excessively long; that the authors of some chronicles devote too little or too much attention to the background of the figure's time; that a third work is overloaded with letters and documents from the man's career. Other exceptions are taken to the subordination of narrative to portraiture and vice versa, to the presentation of only one side of a subject's life, and to the biographer's use of fictional devices. These critical opinions may be well founded. If the work lacks proportion, if the figure is lost to sight in the flow of happenings around him, if the development of character or the progress of the narrative is seriously retarded by the insertion of personal and official papers, there are good grounds for the objections. Before they are counted valid, however, they should be weighed in the light of the biographer's purpose and the kind of biography he has chosen to write.

The personality and career of an individual, and the grist of material that accumulates from his activities, may be treated by various methods and technical principles. Life-literature shows wide differences in the length, content and structure of its units. Biographical writing may be as short as the sketches of lesser figures in the *Dictionary of American Biography*. These pieces contain condensed narratives and certain leading features of their subjects. A biography may be as long as Nicolay and Hay's ten-volume history of Lincoln, which unites the life-narrative and background of the man's time. Among the other types of biography are the conventional work of a single volume, the record which is filled with letters, the life that reads like a novel, and the portrait that is drawn from psychological analysis. Each of these forms presents a man or woman in its own manner.

Although each type has distinct characteristics, the kinds of biographical writing can not be isolated one from the other according to their special qualities. They overlap and merge in their elements. The conventional single volume may specialize in the psychological method; the long chronicle may contain letters and much critical interpretation; the record of letters may have a large segment of the letter-writer's time; the novelized narrative may borrow from psychology. Like the human beings they set forth, the types are both like and unlike. They possess certain features in common—the elements which combine to bring out individuality. They differ on the technical side in the author's selection of material and in his special treatment of the subject matter. Moreover, lives are not written from fixed patterns. Those which properly belong in the same category frequently vary in their qualities, and some works fall between the two kinds. Biographical types, then, are not to be analyzed and pigeonholed in a precise manner.

II

The most common form of biography is the work, usually in one volume, which presents a narrative of the figure's life from birth to death. He is portrayed and interpreted in his various aspects. His achievements or failures in his sphere of activity are described and explained. The man is kept constantly before the reader from the beginning to the end of the narrative. His relation to the events of his time may be explained when that is necessary, but the background of the period is not elaborated. Letters, if used at all, are inserted sparingly and usually only in extracts.

This form of biography frequently becomes a critical study of the figure's achievement, especially if his activity was in one of the fine arts. In this case there is combined with the life-narrative an analysis and appraisal of the person's work. Men of letters, painters and musicians are familiar subjects for studies of this kind.

The regular narrative in one volume has been written most numerously in the United States. A short list of notable examples in the twentieth century follows.

Daniel Boone (1939) by John Bakeless
John C. Calhoun (1950) by Margaret L. Coit
Mark Twain (1943) by DeLancey Ferguson
Winslow Homer (1944) by Lloyd Goodrich
George Washington Carver (1943) by Rackham Holt
The Raven [Sam Houston] (1929) by Marquis James
Henry David Thoreau (1948) by Joseph Wood Krutch
Theodore Roosevelt (1931) by Henry F. Pringle
Baudelaire: Flesh and Spirit (1930) by Lewis P. Shanks
Nathaniel Hawthorne (1948) by Randall Stewart

The pattern of objective biographical writing which blends narrative with more or less portraiture has certain variations which do not specialize in the use of letters, historical background or fictional elements. The single-phase biography treats only one side of the subject's life. Examples are *Washington as a Business Man* (1931) by Halsey L. Ritter, *Lawyer Lincoln* (1937) by Albert A. Woldman, and *Thomas Jefferson, American Tourist* (1946) by Edward Dumbauld.

The other two variants are closely related. In the dual-subject work the author combines the lives of two persons who have been closely connected in one respect or another. *Lewis and Clark: Partners in Discovery* (1947) by John Bakeless illustrates this kind. The multiple-subject or group biography brings together members of the same family. The volumes under this type fall into two divisions. In one part the figures belong to different generations, as in *The Adams Family* (1930) by James Truslow Adams, *The Lees of Virginia* (1935) by Burton J. Hendrick, and *The Lowells and Their Seven Worlds* (1946) by Ferris Greenslet. In the other division the characters are more nearly contemporary, as in *The Doctors Mayo* (1941) by Helen Clapesattle, *The James Family* (1947) by F. O. Mathiessen, *The Peabody Sisters of Salem* (1950) by Louise Hall Tharp, and *The Roosevelt Family of Sagamore Hill* (1954) by Hermann Hagedorn.

III

Some biographers from choice or necessity depict their personages on a broad canvas before the panorama of public events. They combine the "times" with the "life" and unfold the larger affairs of history with the personal adventures of the hero. This double function is a legitimate purpose. In many instances it is a real necessity. The life of an influential individual, as has already been said, can not be cut off from the happenings in which he played a part. He can not be completely separated from the area of society in which he made his impress. This relation of the man to affairs is especially true of leading political figures. It does not apply as strongly to individuals in other fields. The life-and-times type of biography has received critical frowns from those who believe that the author should stick literally to his biographical last. Yet the writer is justified for technical and artistic reasons in depicting his protagonist before a broad background.

The biographer who adopts this form faces a special problem. He must determine how far the ramifications of his hero's life extend in the age, and how much of the period belongs in his work. He must stop the historical portions at the line of relevancy. The chief defect that has appeared in the use of the form lies in an excessive amount of historical matter. A work thus laden is ill-proportioned, the redundant parts impede the narrative, and the central figure may become a subsidiary character in the chronicle. John Marshall's five-volume life of Washington (1804-1807) is deficient in this respect.

Those who defend the use of history with biography may confidently rest their case on the merits of numerous examples. Among these are *Life and Times of Laurence Sterne* (1909) and *History of Henry Fielding* (1918), both by Wilbur L. Cross, *R. E. Lee* (1934, 1935) by Douglas S. Freeman, *Frémont, the West's Greatest Adventurer* (1928) and *Grover Cleveland* (1932), both by Allan Nevins, and *Life and Times of Cavour* (1911) by William Roscoe Thayer. Each of these biographies is in two or more volumes.

Biography of another type is made a vehicle for the correspondence of its central figure. The letters he wrote, as well as some that he received, are inserted in the narrative either in whole or in long extracts. Material of this kind has rich autobiographical value if the letters are illuminating and significant. Besides throwing light on the personality of the writer, letters make clear the viewpoints and opinions of the figure as he originally expressed them. Letters also give his own version of important happenings and critical junctures in his life. They allow him to render firsthand testimony that is not altered by subsequent happenings or colored by later observers. Letters place the figure squarely in the pages of his own biography.

Two objections are advanced to the liberal use of letters in a biography. It is asserted that they impede the progress of the narrative and that they interpose unessential and irrelevant material at points where a sentence or an excerpt would be sufficient. Well written letters that are really informative, however, add substance and vitality to a biography. If the correspondence of the figure were invariably to be excluded from the life, the work would lack the firsthand validation and autobiographic quality whose value has been pointed out. In addition, some readers relish letters and prefer to read them as part of the life-narrative rather than in the collected form of a separate volume. Life-literature has need of a type of biography in which letters may be introduced.

The place of this type is securely fortified by numerous works. Among these are the life and letters of the following: John Greenleaf Whittier (1894) by S. T. Pickard, Oliver Wendell Holmes (1896) by John T. Morse, Jr., Phillips Brooks (1900) by Alexander V. G. Allen, Lafcadio Hearn (1906) by Elizabeth Bisland, Walter Hines Page (1925, 1926) by Burton J. Hendrick, Joseph Pennell (1929) by Elizabeth R. Pennell, Stuart P. Sherman (1929) by Jacob Zeitlin and Homer Woodbridge, and Woodrow Wilson (1927-35) by Ray Stannard Baker.

IV

The novel has been blended with biography in an irregular and variant form which is termed "novelized biography" or "fictional biography" or "biographical novel." These expressions have been loosely used, and they have been broadly applied to all life-narratives of real persons which show the fictional technique and have the air and flavor of the novel. The form in general is also marked by a vividness of character and incident, dramatic action and the illusion of reality. These three qualities, however, are not the exclusive property of fiction. The writer of pure biography may quite properly vitalize his work with them without overstepping the limits of his province. Every life which "reads like a novel" is not a specimen of the fictionalized form. It may be composed solely of pure fact which is given the tone of the novel by the author's skill of imagination.

Opinions differ regarding the exact nature of the novelized biography. The dominant view holds that the true life of this kind must be based wholly on authenticated record. The author should invent nothing—no incidents or characters, conversations, mental workings of his figure, or any other part of his narrative. He simply casts his factual material in the form of the novel. Yet all written lives which are tagged with this label are not devoid of invented matter. The writer of a novelized biography may assert that every line in his book is based on facts which can be verified. This adherence to the record does not necessarily mean that he has written an unimpeachable biography. Has he chosen only the more entertaining and dramatic por tions which more easily afford fictional treatment? Or does the biography embrace the entire range of his subject's life?

The fictional biography is always a mixture of fact and fancy. The author not only draws on firsthand sources or earlier lives of the same figure, he also writes at will without benefit of record and introduces fictive matter as he wishes. He conjectures what his hero may have thought or felt, and said or done, on certain occasions. He lets his imagination furnish details of dress, weather and minor items of all kinds. The assiduous biographer searches far and wide, if it is necessary, for authentic answers to these questions. The fictional writer time and again supplies the answers from his imagination. The fictional biography offers a refuge to the lazy life-writer. It is the joy of the popularizer and the delight of the populace.

The biographical novel, the third variant of the fictionalized form, also contains invented matter. In using this term for his narrative, the author gives fair notice that he is adopting the novel as his basic medium, and he informs the reader at the outset that the latter will enter the quasi realm of the novel. By adopting the biographical method as an accessory device, the author acquires greater freedom in composing his story. This liberty, however, carries no license for him to misrepresent his character. The writer of the biographical novel is the least vulnerable to censure of the ground that he combines the two forms.

There is a kinship between biography and the novel: the former re-creates real men and women in their actual careers, and the latter depicts fictitious characters in their imagined lives. The one demands fidelity to a prototypal record, and the other allows unrestricted play of the imagination. It is not an easy thing to reconcile the requirement of the first with the latitude of the second. The writer who calls himself biographer and adopts the fictionized form can not escape his obligation to the canons of biography even though he claims the privileges of the novel. If he is to serve both arts truly, he must adhere closely to documented fact and at the same time give his narrative the structure and semblance of an imagined work. It is highly difficult to maintain this even adjustment. In actual practice the balance between the two forms is more often lost in favor of the novel.

The legitimacy of the fictionized form has been sharply argued, and biographies written in the manner have been both assailed and applauded. They have been impugned on the ground that they violate the fundamental factual principle of biography. They have been praised for their spirited realism and entertaining quality. With few exceptions, both the indictment and the defense are well founded. The case hinges primarily on the question of whether a biographer has the right to add to or omit from the factual record of the original life in order to obtain the likeness of a novel in his narrative. Has he the right (a) to insert thoughts, conversations and incidents that are pure invention; (b) to transpose the time-order of happenings; (c) to deliberately exclude facts which hinder his fictional purpose?

In answering these questions, the nature of biography must be considered. The biographer deals with material which in effect is evidence, testimony and proof. He is always a witness, sometimes a judge, and even, in rare instances, a prosecutor. In any of these roles he is bound by his art to use as his data only the established truth, so far as that can be ascertained. Fictional matter weakens the biographic legality of his work. The argument has been advanced that a biographer may properly employ invention if the fictional parts are in harmony with the spirit of his subject's life. This principle is repugnant to the rule of biographical evidence. In its operation, moreover, it has the great defect of being vague. The requisite of "harmony" actually puts small restraint on the inventive faculty of the biographer. Wild flights of fancy and picturesque concoctions may agree with the tenor of a person's life. An extenuating circumstance exists when the author makes clear the parts of his narrative which are invented. If this is done, the reader can at least separate the fiction from the fact and draw his own conclusions. The lover of the truth may demand with reason that the author's imagination not impair the genuineness of the record that is reproduced. The person who is indifferent to the biographic truth gives aid and comfort to the fictionist. Biography does not need the expedient of invention for the effective re-creation of its characters. This is proved by the absence of the device from great works.

The novelized form with its variants was a product of the biographic agitation of the 1920s. The fictional idea, however, had served biography long before that time. In the early years of the nineteenth century Mason Locke Weems had invented freely in his lives of Washington (1806) and General Francis Marion (1809). "Knowing the passion of the times for novels," Weems wrote, "I have endeavored to throw . . . ideas and facts about General Marion into the garb of a military romance." Despite his great success with his readers, Weems inspired no followers who might easily have adopted his strange methods and improved upon them. For a hundred years American biographers adhered to the classic tradition of their art and ignored the beguiling devices of fiction.

When Mark Twain wrote his *Personal Recollections of*

Joan of Arc (1896), he wove the historical facts into a pattern of fictional narrative and embellished them with all the vigor of his imagination. This method was characteristic of the man. Ingrained storyteller that he was, Clemens could never have held himself to the limits of a factual record. Moreover, in writing the life of the Maid he was fired with anger at the evils of her time and inspired by an adoration of his heroine. As a tribute to his ideal of womanhood the book commands respect. As fictionalized biography the life humanizes its figure effectively and does no serious harm to historical evidence. The embroidery which accompanies the facts is frequently unreal, showy and excessive.

Gertrude Atherton was a pioneer worker in the kind of biographical fiction that flourished in the 1920s. In writing a life of Alexander Hamilton, which was entitled *The Conqueror,* and published in 1902, Mrs. Atherton discarded the conventional form of presenting her hero and drew the portrait with the freedom of the independent novelist that she was. She adorned the biographical framework of Hamilton's career with the accessories of romantic fiction, and so freely did she use these trappings that they dominated the narrative. Although the book embodied wide reading and research by the author, the actual record underwent considerable change before Mrs. Atherton's imagination and invention. The result was a highly entertaining but unreliable biography which worshipped its hero, but did him injustice by playing up the quasi romantic happenings in his life and subordinating or omitting matters of less interest to uncritical readers. Mrs. Atherton achieved a dubious technical success and a positive financial success, but she began no new school of fictional biographers.

The Conqueror is typical of one species of fictional biography, but it is by no means representative of the whole genus. Far superior to Mrs. Atherton's book are several later biographies which employ fictional elements in greater or less degree without damage to the essential nature of their characters. These re-created lives have a convincing reality. They make the figures known as those individuals were and as they lived in actual existence. The portraits are rounded and are not limited to striking features chosen for dramatic effect. If the narratives are embroidered, lightly or heavily, with items and incidents that are imagined or invented, the fictional embellishments are partly or wholly —depending on the reader's taste—counterbalanced by the incontestable virtues of the books.

The volumes which are listed here are not cut to the same pattern. Each author has followed his or her own method in using the fictional devices. Among the biographies which belong in the superior group of this type are: *R. v. R. The Life and Times of Rembrandt van Rijn* (1930) by Hendrik Willem van Loon, *Immortal Wife* (Jessie Benton Frémont) (1944) by Irving Stone, *The Life of Margaret Fuller* (1942) by Madeleine B. Stern, and *Yankee from Olympus: Justice Holmes and His Family* (1944) and *John Adams and the American Revolution* (1950), both by Catherine Drinker Bowen.

In "A Word about Sources and Methods" in *John Adams,* Mrs. Bowen writes in part: ". . . 'Fictionalized biography' is the current label. I myself do not admit a phrase which, besides being doubtful English, does not express what I am trying to do. Call it, rather, a portrait of John Adams. I have drawn a portrait and like Saint Mémin I have used the *physionotrace;* I have found instruments with which to measure and then I have gone ahead and painted. In brief, I studied the available evidence and, on the basis of it, built pictures which to me are consistent with the evidence."

V

The short biography differs from the long life chiefly in the matter of length. It likewise divides into various categories. It comprises all the technical elements which are found in the extended biography. These elements, which may be recalled here, are narrative, descriptive, analytic, explanatory, interpretative and critical. As in the case of the long works, all biographies that are written in the reduced length do not contain all these elements. A short life may be purely narrative, or it may consist of a combination of certain elements. One kind of short account, however, has no counterpart in the classes of long biographies: that is the treatment which is solely character analysis. The short biography also employs practically the same material as the long work, although letters are rarely used except in brief excerpts, and background matter is usually excluded for reasons of length.

The short biography is so diversified in content, structrue and length that no absolute division of its various classes can be made. An attempted classification would inevitably leave many condensed lives unlabelled or consigned to that convenient catchall, the miscellaneous group. Yet the nature of the short biography appears more definitely when one examines the different kinds and their chief qualities.

The longer classes of the short biography are the abridged form of the conventional life, two divisions of the essay, the memoir, and the portrait and its allied forms, which are the psychograph and the profile.

All these types are essays in effect. Each one is a relatively short treatment of a single topic. Each is complete in itself, yet "incomplete" in the essay sense in that the author does not exhaust the possibilities of his subject. Short biographies may be written in a formal or an informal manner. They may be compact or loose in organization; serious or humorous in tone; conventional or original in the way in which the author presents his subject. Some short biographies are written objectively, but the greater number of them are more or less revelatory of the writer.

VI

Biographical length being a matter of scale, many authors have chosen to use a form which resembles the strict or conventional biography in practically everything except length. The type is narrative in structure, extending from the birth or earlier years of the figure to his later years or death. More selective in its subject matter than the long work, the abridged form contains the main and significant happenings in the man's life, it traces the course of his career, and it describes his personal characteristics. It may or may not have the critical estimates of the writer. This type is also one kind of biographical essay. It is a life history in miniature. Examples are the essays on Franklin, Poe and Daniel Webster in the *Dictionary of American Biography*.

There are two classes of biographical essays. The first, which has just been described, contains a rounded account of its subject. The second kind presents a selective treatment of its figure. It has little or no narrative and dwells on character and manifestations of character rather than on external happenings. In using this method, the author centers his attention on one or more aspects of the man and discusses his subject from a particular point of view. He chooses the qualities which are relevant to his purpose and omits other matter. This type of essay is written in the subjective manner. It lights up the personality of the author himself, revealing his convictions and his considered attitude toward his figure.

Examples of the selective biographical essay are those on Thoreau and Lincoln by James Russell Lowell, the discussions of Thoreau and Hawthorne by Paul Elmer More in *Shelburne Essays,* and the heroes whom Emerson portrayed in *Representative Men.* The essay on Thoreau by Emerson is also a work of this type, but it is much less subjective than the usual character essay.

VII

The memoir is written from the firsthand knowledge and personal experience of the author. He has known his figure at near view in actual life and has often been more or less closely associated with the man. This element of acquaintance or friendship is the chief distinguishing characteristic of the memoir. The skillful biographer who is able to draw accurately on his memory and uses his knowledge and impressions judiciously gives his account the tone of familarity and authority. The memoir frequently has a strain of appreciation, which may range from quiet restraint to uninhibited culogy. The memoir may have a methodical or a rambling arrangement of its material.

Biographical writing in this country began in the form of the memoir. (See Chapter II under *Practice.*) A later, and excellent, example of the short memoir is the address on Henry David Thoreau which Emerson gave at the funeral of his friend in May, 1862, and which was afterward published in an expanded form. The fine appreciation, *My Mark Twain* (1910), which William Dean Howells wrote of his humorist friend, has the qualities of a memoir.

The word has also been applied to full-length biographies which follow the pattern of the conventional long life. Oliver Wendell Holmes, senior, composed *Memoir of John Lothrop Motley* (1879), and *A Memoir of Ralph Waldo Emerson* (1887) was written in two volumes by James E. Cabot. These works are both biographies in the ordinary sense. The term has been further used in the plural to designate conventional biographies as well as autobiographical accounts. The varied application of the word furnishes an instance of the lack of uniformity in the use of biographical nomenclature.

The term appeared often in the titles of life-records in the nineteenth century, but it has now disappeared almost completely from titular designations. To some minds it suggests a dead biographical fashion and obsolete volumes on dusty shelves. Articles and books which are memoirs in effect are still written, notably in the manner of as-I-knew-him and as-he-was biographies. A memoir literature has grown up around the life and career of Franklin D. Roosevelt.

VIII

A biographical portrait is a study in character. It aims to tell what a man or woman is or was. It presents an analysis of the distinguishing qualities of a person—those attributes which stamp his particular individuality and differentiate him from other human beings. The writer of the portrait examines the words and acts and creative work of his subject for manifestations of character, and knits his findings into a unified word-picture. In his delineation he may follow the chronological order of happenings in his figure's life, or he may arrange the personal qualities in any convenient form which achieves clearness and completeness.

The maker of a biographical portrait undertakes a most difficult task. During the course of his life a man produces an infinite mass of evidence on his character. From this the biographer must select not only the essential points, but also the instances which are representative as well as exceptional, and which in the aggregate will furnish a true and rounded portrait. He must know thoroughly the setting of his figure's career and must weigh the circumstances in which each piece of evidence appears. He must try to understand the meaning and significance of the revelations of character, and he must endeavor to interpret them for his own satisfaction if not for the enlightenment of the reader. If he enlarges his field of research and consults the testimony of relatives, associates and other students of his subject, he frequently meets discrepant statements and contradictory assertions. For all these reasons the portrait becomes a distinctly subjective product.

The biographical portrait and the character sketch resemble each other to a great degree, and the terms are much alike in their meaning and implications. The portrait is often the longer of the two types, and it is more likely to have the narrative arrangement. A greater difference, which exists more in theory than in practice, is the depth of treatment. The writer of the portrait is apt to go further in analyzing his figure. He has a tendency to search for causes and motives for utterances and behavior and to make conjectures and deductions. Before the latter part of the nineteenth century, the sketch was almost wholly devoid of these things. Now it frequently reflects the analytic spirit which has affected biography in general. Many writers, ignoring a technical label, develop their study as they see fit and title it with the name of the subject or with a graphic descriptive phrase

Short pieces in which character was emphasized over narrative have long been a part of biographical literature. Plutarch's lives were character sketches. The writers of the early memoirs in New England dwelt on the inner qualities of their worthies. The sketch is old, but the portrait, as a distinct form, was created in the nineteenth century. It came into American biography from the work of the French author, Charles Augustin Sainte-Beuve (1804-1869). By profession Sainte-Beuve was a literary critic, but to him criticism was a study of character as that was revealed in literature. His method was "to go straight at the author under the mask of the book." He dissected the product of the writer to discover the nature of the man. "J'analyze, j'herborize, je suis un naturaliste des esprits," he said. The pursuit of his goal led him deep into the human being. He then wrote a psychological study in which he used the narrative arrangement of his subject's life. Sainte-Beuve did not confine his attention to literary people. He also depicted artists, soldiers, statesmen and other types of men and women. In all, he set forth some seven hundred individuals. His essay on Benjamin Franklin is one of the best characterizations of that American in existence. Sainte-Beuve gave the term *portrait* to his studies. The word has been applied in American biography to a wide variety of character analyses and word-pictures. Some of these resemble the work of Sainte-Beuve in their method and result; others bear little or no relation to his technique.

Gamaliel Bradford, a disciple of Sainte-Beuve and the most distinguished writer of portraits in the United States, objected to that term, although he used it out of consideration for the exigencies of publication. Bradford said that it was misleading to carry the terms of one art into another. A biographical portraitist, he explained, could depict the character of a man "in only one phase, one situation, one set of conditions and circumstances." He preferred to call his studies of individuals *psychographs,* and he maintained that the aim of psychography is opposite to that of portraiture. (Bradford and his work are further considered in Chapter XIII under *Practice.*)

The profile is the candid-camera variant of the biographical portrait. As it was developed in a long series of sketches in *The New Yorker,* in which magazine the term originated, the profile has specialized in drawing men and women whose personalities and careers are clearly defined, sharply individualized and conspicuously out of the ordinary. The figures have been unconventional, unusual, atypical. Persons who are colorless or conventional are not good subjects for the profile. The various writers of the profiles have shown most interest in the features and incidents which illustrate the striking qualities and colorful singularity of their subjects. The style of the profile has been facile, brisk, concrete. Among the persons who have been etched in this form are Vincent Astor ("The Golden Spoon"), Father Divine ("Who Is This King of Glory?"), and Nicholas Murray Butler ("Cosmos").

IX

The biographical sketch is a still shorter form of the condensed life. It is slighter in construction than the essay. It is a brief account which contains the main features of the subject's life and often includes mention of his personal qualities. The sketch is found in biographical dictionaries and literary anthologies.

The biographical notice is a short narrative statement containing a limited number of essential facts about a person's life. The notice often serves to identify a musician, a painter or a writer. It may or may not have critical comment. Notices of this kind are frequently printed in concert programs and lists of museum exhibits and in the contributors-to-this-issue columns of periodicals.

BOOK II: THE PRACTICE OF AMERICAN BIOGRAPHY

CHAPTER I

THE BIOGRAPHIC IMPULSE IN
THE COLONIAL HISTORIES

The beginnings of American biography lie in the pages of colonial literature. Before lives of individual men were written and printed in separate form, the impulse to biography appeared in the chronicles of the earliest settlements in New England. These narratives came into existence primarily from the historical motive,—from the feeling held by serious-minded men that the venture of colonization and the business of living in the new world should have permanent record. In writing their chronicles they dwelt on the group-life of the communities rather than the sequence of happenings in the lives of the single members. No drama, however, can be unfolded without heed of the players, and the early histories are filled with passages which describe the inner qualities of men and women as well as their external acts. The passages are in the nature of brief observations which afford insight into character, small segments of uncompleted portrayals, and fragmentary episodes of human enterprise. They are the first indications of life-literature written in the English language on American soil. They form the prelude to the great body of American biography.

William Bradford, in writing the history of the Plymouth Colony from 1630 to 1650, wove into his narrative brief characterizations of men who had figured in the affairs of the settlement. He refers to the service performed by Governor John Carver, "a man godly and well approved amongst them." He describes the difficulty in the matter of religion which the colony had with Roger Williams, "a man godly and zealous, having many precious parts, but very unsettled in judgment." A few pages are devoted to Thomas Morton, the troublesome neighbor at Merry Mount, and an "unworthy man, and instrument of mischief." These are but faint signs of portraiture. More indicative of the biographic impulse is the sketch of the life of William Brewster, which comprises eighteen hundred words and is by far the longest account of a single individual in Bradford's history. Brewster was head of the church at Plymouth for many years. Bradford wrote of his friend in simple and temperate language and with quiet appreciation of Brewster's qualities.

The *Journal* which John Winthrop kept of the colony at Massachusetts Bay contains no long passages like the sketch of Brewster. When he mentioned men and women, however, Winthrop was inclined, even more than Bradford, to add brief estimates of their characters. His *Journal* is filled with such expressions as "a godly man and a prime scholar," "a wise and godly gentleman," and "a godly young woman and of special parts." A longer description accompanied the notice of the death of "that faithful servant of the Lord, Mr. Thomas Hooker, pastor of the church in Hartford, who, for piety, prudence, wisdom, zeal, learning, and what else might make him serviceable in the place and time he lived in, might be compared with men of greatest note. . . ."

After the death of William Bradford, the manuscript of his history, which had not been published, passed into the hands of his nephew, Nathaniel Morton, who was secretary of the Plymouth Colony for forty years. Morton made extensive use of the document, with acknowledgment to his uncle, in compiling another history, entitled *New England's Memorial* (published in 1669). In his work Morton took special pains to commemorate members of both the colonies at Plymouth and Massachusetts Bay. The chief additions which he made to the contents of Bradford's chronicle were biographical and obituary notices.

Edward Johnson sounded the virtues of the Puritans in vigorous terms in *The Wonder-Working Providence of Zion's Saviour in New England* (published in London in 1654). Johnson's history extended from 1628 to 1651. Throughout the narrative he poured forth abundant praise for the leading laymen and divines. John Endicott was "a fit instrument to begin this wilderness-work, of courage bold undaunted, yet sociable, and of cheerful spirit, loving and austere, applying himself to either as occasion served." Richard Mather was "the sage, grave, reverend and faithful servant of Christ;" he was "indued by the Lord with many heavenly gifts, of a plain and upright spirit, apt to teach, full of gracious expressions, and resolvedly bent to follow the truth, as it is in Jesus."

Until the middle of the seventeenth century the biographic element existed only in the histories. It then emerged from the pages of the chroniclers in the expanded form of the memoir. Dissociated from the purely historical motive, the biographic tendency passed into a separate and independent development.*

---

*Historical writing has, of course, continued to have the biographic strain, the extent of which has depended on the historian's treatment of his material. Much biography, especially that of the life-and-times kind, has likewise contained an admixture of history.

CHAPTER II

THE COLONIAL PERIOD (1658-1790)

A peculiar interest lies in books that were the first of their kind in point of time. Whatever their intrinsic worth, or their rank in later criticism, they possess a certain significance because of their priority. In this respect the memoirs of the Colonial period have three noteworthy features. They mark the transition in life-writing from the old world to the new. They denote the nature of the inheritance with which the first biographers on these shores began their work. They show American biography in its elementary stage, and they contain certain characteristics which were to appear in later times in more extended and involved lives. For these reasons it is well to pause for a while with the memoirists and their worthies.

John Cotton, Puritan divine of Boston, died in December of 1652. "The lectures in his church, the whole winter following, performed by the neighboring ministers, were but so many funeral sermons upon the death and worth of this extraordinary person."[1] The eulogies of Cotton even-

---

[1] Cotton Mather, "Life of John Cotton" in *Magnalia Christi Americana*, Vol. I, p. 273.

tually culminated in a printed memoir which bore the title: *The Life and Death of the Deservedly Famous Mr. John Cotton, Late Reverend Teacher of the Church of Christ in Boston.* The author was John Norton, who had become Cotton's successor at the First Church. The memoir was printed in a volume of fifty-one pages at Cambridge, Massachusetts, and was dated 1658.[2] It was the first life-account to be published in the form of a separate book in the colonies.[3]

John Cotton was the perfect subject for the first Puritan biography. He was ranked by the early settlers of Boston as foremost among them. For nineteen years he occupied a position of high authority in the theocracy of Massachusetts.

The memoir was written in the language of an erudite sermon and fervent eulogy. "They who have known his doctrine, manner of life, purpose, faith, long-suffering, love, patience, persecutions, and affliction," the author testified, "do not suffer such a Light to be hid under a bushel, but put it on a candlestick, that it may give light to them that are in the House."

Norton began the memoir with an explanation of his reasons for writing. A memorial of a godly man, he said, is favored with a divine and special benediction. To suppress an instrument of so much good would be not only an act of ingratitude to the dead, but an injury to the present and

---

[2]This was eighteen years after the printing of the "Bay Psalm Book," the first book to be printed in English in America, and twenty-eight years after the Massachusetts Bay Colony was established. Cotton was a member of this colony. The Pilgrims had landed at Plymouth thirty-eight years before the memoir was published.

---

[3]In the seventeenth and eighteenth centuries in America, the term *biography* was not applied to memoirs and other life-accounts. It is used in this chapter to designate works which, by the later use of the word, are biographical in nature. The term and its cognates are rarely found in American writing before the nineteenth century. John Dryden, as has been said, introduced the word *biography* into the English language in 1683.

to future generations. Makers of memorials perform a three-fold function: they preserve the excellence of the dead, they continue the memory of their friends, and they give testimony to what the faithful have done and suffered.

The memoir is composed of nearly equal parts of biography, eulogy and sermon. The biographical portion is a framework overlaid with moralizing passages and embellished with laudatory phrases. John Norton quite accurately considered his work a memorial. His purpose was to commemorate an eminent colleague and to preserve a high ideal for others to strive after. Besides paying tribute to the deceased divine, he also desired to perform a service for the church. It is small wonder that in the face of these aims he should convert the plain facts of John Cotton's life into a work of hagiography.*

Another leading clergyman, Richard Mather, was commemorated in a memoir composed by his son Increase and published (1670) under the title: *The Life and Death of That Reverend Man of God, Mr. Richard Mather, Teacher of the Church in Dorchester in New-England.* This life differs in several respects from Norton's memoir. It lacks the eulogistic and sermonic elements of the earlier work, and is written in a more objective manner. The tone is reverential, the style simple and unadorned. In a brief introduction Increase Mather, who was also a divine, adduced the benefits to readers of written lives of worthy men. He then related the narrative of his father's life, to which he added a modest character portrayal, He closed the memoir with Richard Mather's will and testament.

The most voluminous writer of lives in the Colonial time was Cotton Mather, who belonged to the third generation

*From "The First American Biography" by Dana K. Merrill in *The New England Quarterly,* Vol. XI, pp. 152-154, March, 1938.

of his famous family. Mather was, in effect, the official biographer of early New England Puritanism. Ten years before his death, his son Samuel says, Cotton Mather had published the lives of no less than one hundred and fourteen men and more than twenty women. He added to the number in his last years. Most of these accounts, however, while they vary in length, are comparable in scope to the articles in the present-day biographical dictionaries.

Mather's *magnum opus* was the *Magnalia Christi Americana*, or "The Ecclesiastical History of New England" (London, 1702). This was a large omnibus volume which contained much miscellany Mather had published before. "The great object of the first Planters of New-England," he wrote in the preface, was to form a Christian Commonwealth," and one of the reasons for the publication of the history was "that the names of such eminent persons as the Lord made use of, as instruments in his hand, for the beginning and carrying on of this work, may be embalmed, and preserved, for the knowledge and imitation of posterity." Among its contents the *Magnalia* contains accounts of some sixty divines and eight governers of the colonies. Representative of Mather as a biographer are the lives of John Cotton and Thomas Hooker of the clergymen, and William Bradford, John Winthrop and Sir William Phips of the governors.

Cotton Mather's biographies were the work of a clergyman-scholar of boundless erudition who wrote as he lived— with all his Puritan might. In the General Introduction of the *Magnolia* he set forth the principles by which the book was composed. He did not think of his lives as belonging to a separate branch of writing. He made no distinction in his critical exposition between history and biography, and he seems to have considered the lives an intrinsic part of the historical record.[4]

Mather stated that he had passed judgment of praise and blame upon his characters, but when this was done honestly, he maintained, it was the rightful function of a historian. Yet he considered it his duty "to be more sparing and easie" in mentioning "censurable things." He defended this procedure with the argument that "It is not the Work of an Historian, to commemorate the Vices and Villainies of men, as much as their just, their fair, their honest Actions: And the Readers of History get more good by the Objects of their Emulation, than of their Indignation." Mather added that he had "left unmentioned some censurable occurrences in story of our colonies, as things" useless and "improper to be raised out of the grave, wherein oblivion hath now buried them."

Cotton Mather thus weighed his characters in the scales of his own values. He assumed the right to minimize or suppress certain traits and acts of his figures and to emphasize those things which, in his opinion, would benefit his readers spiritually and morally. The viewpoint which he took toward the portrayal of his characters was to be adopted by many biographers in the eighteenth and nineteenth centuries. The later authors took the position of their own accord and not as disciples of the Puritan historian.

Mather declared that he had composed his biographies "with all Conscience of Truth." The reader soon learns that he saw the truth in the warm light of eulogy. "How can

---

[4]An instance of the early use of the word *biography* in an American colonial book is in the *Magnalia*. *Mather* wrote in the General Introduction: "I add hereunto, the Notables of the only Protestant University, that ever shone in that Hemisphere of the New World; with particular Instances of Criolians, in our Biography, provoking the whole World, with vertuous Objects of Emulation." (Criolians is "an obsolete word for persons born or naturalized in America, but of European race.")

the Lives of the Commendable be written without Commending them?" he asked. The general plan of his book embraced only men whom he could sincerely praise. Rogues and sinners were outside the compass of his biographic purpose unless they could be held up as moral objects by their misdeeds. There was no need of charcoal in writing the lives of those who had labored so earnestly in the service of God and for the welfare of their fellow-men. "If he does not tell just what men were," a biographer of Cotton Mather writes, "he does tell just what they wanted to be, and what loyal posterity longed to believe them."[5]

The colonial memoir which meets best the test of present twentieth-century standards is *The Life and Character of the Reverend Benjamin Colman* (Boston, 1749). This was written by Ebenezer Turell, who was Colman's son-in-law and also a minister. Turell said that he had tried to avoid the conventional type portrait of a clergyman and to individualize his subject. In this attempt he was successful to a degree uncommon at that time.[6] The first seven chapters of the book contain the narrative of Colman's career. The next chapter deals with his labors in his profession, and the following section gives a view of his private life. The final chapter is a miscellany which includes the circumstances of his death, a tribute by President Holyoke of Harvard, and a list of Colman's published works.

Although the account is uniformly favorable to its subject,

[5]Barrett Wendell, *Cotton Mather: Puritan Priest*, p. 161.

---

[6]In the preface of his book Turell wrote: "I hope I have been preserved in a good Measure from that Error which many Biographers and Eulogists insensibly slide into in Narratives of this kind, scil. Making their Subject to excell in every Thing, by drawing a perfect Character (as of a good Magistrate, Minister, &c.) without showing us the Man, scil. those particular excelling Qualities which distinguish him from others." This is another of the rare instances in which *biography* is found in American writing of the eighteenth century.

it lacks the eulogistic and sermonic elements, and possesses the great virtue of being concretely informative. The compiler of who's who data would find Turell's work of real value. He would learn even the streets on which Dr. Colman lived in Boston. This memoir comes nearest of the colonial lives to being "pure" biography.

From the beginning, with Norton's memoir of Cotton in 1658, until the Revolution, biography in the New England colonies was written almost entirely by clergymen. The high standing which the divines had in the communities, together with their learning, made them the logical biographers of their colonial society. The memoirists were few in number, and with the exception of Cotton Mather they rarely extended their work in this field. For the most part they turned only for the moment to commemorate a relative or a friend. The figures they depicted were of three types: other clergymen, lay persons whose spiritual excellence had impressed them, and men who had held civil office. The contemporary readers of the memoirs did not go to them for mere information. The readers sought solace and inspiration, and communion with great souls in their history. The colonial biographies were much shorter than the lives of the nineteenth and twentieth centuries. A comprehensive narrative from birth to death, with ample detail and proportion, was unknown. Much was condensed and omitted. The memoirs contained personal anecdotes, letters, documents and directly quoted remarks.

The colonial biographers were the first heirs of Plutarch in the new world. They mentioned him in their narratives, and his spirit hovered over their desks as they composed their resolute memorials. Their accounts show two other strains of influence, the Gospels of the New Testament and the lives of the early Christian saints. The memoirists carried on the traditions of portraiture which had sprung from religious and classical sources. In commemorating their worthies as a matter of historical record, the colonial authors also sought to make them the objects of emulation. The moralizing element found strong response in the Anglo-Saxon nature, and it was strengthened by the Puritan doctrine, which interpreted life in terms of moral values. The divines also felt that through their memoirs they were performing a service to the glory of God. Biography in America thus originated from the historical, eulogistic, ethical and devotional motives.

The Revolution terminated the era of colonial memoirs. Before 1790 life-literature in the form of biography was confined almost entirely to New England. In the other colonies persons kept diaries and journals and wrote autobiographical narratives, but little inclination was shown to record the lives of others as part of historical chronicles.

Chapter III

BIOGRAPHY IN THE NEW NATION
(1790-1830)

The small stream of memorials which flowed gently through New England literature in the Colonial time began to widen into a strong current after the nation was founded. During the first half of the nineteenth century biography in the United States had a vigorous growth. It was practised eagerly, but not always skillfully, and it brought into its volumes a multitude of characters.

During those years biographical literature developed under the influence of three powerful factors. The first of these, which was born in the struggle for independence. was the spirit of hero-worship that thrilled with the sense of victory and the recognition of the victors' achievement. The second factor was a desire for a culture that would be expressive of the United States. The written record of men's careers in various spheres of activity offered tangible evidence of such a culture. The new national feeling which led the poets and novelists to begin the creation of a native liter ature likewise stirred the men who turned to biography. The third force lay in the traditional principles of life-writing which had been brought from the old world to the New England colonies and were carried on after the Revolution. The effect of these factors appears in biographical literature down to the mid-century.

The memoirists of the Colonial era had, as it were, built a little sanctuary for their saints. The hero-worshippers of the early nineteenth century constructed an imposing pantheon for their deities. Biography in the new nation began in the midst of the reverberations of the war and the deliberations of state-making. The men who played parts in those events became the inevitable subjects of biographers in whom the commemorative purpose was reinforced by the patriotic motive.

Washington was, quite appropriately, the first hero to be celebrated in the new pantheon. The biography that placed him there--the first life to be published in the United States after his death in 1799--did not befit the man or the occasion, yet it outlived nobler tributes to the president. In its original edition (1800) the biography was a pamphlet of eighty pages, a concoction turned out by an itinerant bookseller who was bent on quick sales to a mourning country. The author, Mason Locke Weems, needs no introduction today. The story of Weems--his picturesque personality, lively adventures and odd books--has been told times without end. Few writers have ever treated the life of Washington without taking notice, in jest, earnest or scorn, of his first biographer. Once a collecter of folk tales, he himself has become a folk figure, and his life of Washington a folk book. He is the center of an episode that is firmly imbedded in a great tradition.

As an author Weems was an alert diagnostician of the

popular taste who skillfully blended sentiment, morality and patriotism in entertaining narratives. It is a commonplace that he planted in the popular mind a concept of Washington which clung for decades. The impression still persists in some quarters. Weems launched the familiar legend with its story of the cherry tree and other anecdotes. The legend grew from a later edition of the biography rather than from the original pamphlet. Spurred by the success of the first small book, Weems embarked on new and enlarged versions. The fifth edition (1806)—*A Life of George Washington, With Curious Anecdotes, Honorable to Himself and Exemplary to His Young Countrymen*—portrayed the hero at greater length and contained the well-known stories. The actual origin of the tales is uncertain. One conjecture holds that they had already been told of other men and were applied to Washington by Weems in order to add lustre to his figure.

The book is a mixture of biography, fiction, folklore and tract. Weems was no scholar, aiming to present only authentic matter. If he did seek facts, he was not halted in his work by lack of them. With him fancy took the place of document. His sources were frequently hearsay and tradition. Weems did not seek solely to entertain his readers. He wanted to teach them as well,—to show them that Washington's "rise and elevation were owing to his Great Virtues." The biography is inlaid with a heavy strain of moral instruction. Weems said in his preface that he was writing for children. He composed his narrative in a loose form of the novel. Although the hero was highly idealized, he was intensely alive to the readers of that period. The biography is, in short, a story of service and success, spun in an engaging fashion on the loom of patriotism.

Weems also wrote lives of General Francis Marion (1809),

Benjamin Franklin (1817) and William Penn (1819). In the genus of life-writers he belongs with the fabricators of fictional biography. He was the people's biographer of his time. His books were reprinted in countless editions, and they continued to be read long after his death in 1825. American autobiography would have gained a unique volume if Parson Weems had put himself, his adventures "on the road," and his knowledge of native folkways into a narrative of his own life.

The official life of Washington was written by John Marshall, who became chief justice in 1801. The work was undertaken at the request of Washington's nephew Bushrod, who had inherited the papers of the late president. Marshall was a staunch Federalist, and had known Washington, and the idea of writing the life of his leader appealed to him both as a matter of sentiment and a means of financial profit. Great jurist though he was, Marshall did not have the temperament of a historian or the skill of a biographer. He and Bushrod Washington planned a biography of four or five volumes, and as his toil proceeded Marshall was irked by the laborious research and prolonged writing which the project required. The work was issued in five volumes at intervals from 1804 to 1807.

Rather than being a biography in the strict sense, the book was more a history with special attention to the life of Washington. Marshall dwelt at great length with men and events that made up the Revolution and the founding of the nation. He treated political parties, the military system, social and economic conditions, and foreign affairs. Much of this matter would be pertinent in a biography of the life-and-times kind, which Marshall's work really was, but the author enlarged upon these phases of his history more extensively than was necessary. As a result the book suffered badly from lack of proportion. The work as a whole was also marred by factual errors and faulty composition. The defective structure of the biography was caused largely by Marshall's use of scores of passages that were borrowed bodily from other books. Marshall admitted that he had copied extensively from other authors. By present-day standards of scholarship he did not make adequate acknowledgment of these sources.[1]

With these borrowings, or in spite of them, Marshall's work was better as history than biography. Official though the life was intended to be, and abundant as was the material that was used, the narrative was wanting in points of pure fact, and it lacked sufficient details of important episodes in Washington's career. The author knew his figure well enough to make a lifelike portrait. He possessed, as parts of the biography show, the qualities of sympathy, fairness and restraint. The portrait was temperate in tone and not lavish in eulogy. Marshall's treatment of his hero was formal and stately. In the twentieth century the delineation has been likened to a marble statue and a steel engraving. The last volume of the series closed with an analysis of Washington's character which, says Marshall's biographer, Albert J. Beveridge, came to be the conventional estimate of the man.

Marshall later (1832) published a corrected edition of the whole history. The revised version was much superior to the first. In it he rectified errors, improved the composition and condensed parts of the original edition. As time went on, the deficiencies of the first edition were forgotten before the merits of the corrected version, which was

---

[1]Marshall's indebtedness to other works is analyzed and the charge of plagiarism is discussed in an article by William A. Foran, "John Marshall as a Historian" in *American Historical Review*, Vol. XLIII, pp. 51-64, October 1937. There is a short discussion of Marshall's life of Washington as a "composite work" in Allan Nevins, *The Gateway to History*, pp. 159-155.

still some distance from being correct. The authorized life of Washington did not become official in the minds of his countrymen.[2]

The lives of Weems and Marshall began a line of books which converted the first president into a national deity. During the next fifty years biographers idealized Washington, exalting his virtues as a man, a military leader and a statesman, allowing him few ordinary attributes and admitting no faults in their portrayals. To his contemporaries Washington had been a real person. To immediate posterity he became a sanctified figure. These biographies were both a cause and an effect. They made Washington a superhuman and consecrated hero, and at the same time they reflected the sentiment which already existed through the country. People venerated him, and the biographes confirmed their convictions.

Many other political and military figures of the Revolutionary era were commemorated by one or more writers in the first half of the nineteenth century. Lives were published of Jefferson, Hamilton, Franklin, Patrick Henry, Lafayette, John Paul Jones, James Otis, Nathanael Greene and others. None of these men had a popularizer like Weems to spread a lasting legend among the people or an official sculptor to match Marshall's statue of Washington. These biographies performed a needed service in telling the American people about their historical figures, but with few exceptions the books did not live beyond the generation in which they were written.[3]

---

[2]A long account of Marshall's biography is in Albert J. Beveridge, *The Life of John Marshall*, Vol. III, Ch. V, pp. 223-273.

---

[3]Weems' life of Franklin was widely read among the plain people, but Weems either copied from the *Autobiography* word for word or approximated Franklin's phraseology. Through the *Autobiography* Franklin was his own "popularizer" in the early nineteenth century. Weems' life of General Marion was also a favorite biography at this time.

The zeal in hero-worship rose to new heights in *Sketches of the Life and Character of Patrick Henry* (1817), which was written by William Wirt, a powerful orator himself and a distinguished lawyer of Virginia. As a biography the book is fragmentary and incomplete. The material for a life of Henry was meager, there were few records to draw on, and Wirt was forced to rely chiefly on traditional matter and the verbal testimony of persons who had known his hero. He stretched his slender account of Henry's life over a historical framework of the time and inserted numerous digressions of his own on sundry subjects. Wirt exceeded the traditional eloquence of Henry's speeches with the fervor of his own eulogy of the man. "Henry was Shakespeare and Garrick combined," he declared. A great cataract was "like Homer and Henry." A critic who reviewed the biography wrote: "Not only the grandest objects in nature, but the greatest men that ever lived are gravely marshaled into similes and other figures of speech to illustrate this notable idol of his imagination."[4]

The speeches which had made Patrick Henry famous did not exist in verbatim form. Relying again on the same sources of information and using his own power of invention, Wirt re-created the lost speeches in a style that befitted the renown of the fiery orator of the Virginia Assembly. In this way the biographer wrote the "give me liberty, or give me death" speech, which quickly became a classic in the realm of oratory. Wirt's biography is remembered more for this masterpiece than for anything else.

II

The charge of hero-worship has been a repeated com-

---

[4]Jared Sparks in the *North American Review*, Vol. VI, p. 293, March 1818. Sparks belonged to the hero-worshipping school of the period but he disapproved of Wirt's excessive praise.

plaint against the early biographers of the Revolutionary figures. The fault of the authors was not in their veneration of the subjects but in their lack of the critical attitude. They were memorialists engaged in building a pantheon, rather than naturalists of human beings. They wrote their books in the mood of an address which is delivered at a rite of dedication. On such occasions the judicial faculty is inclined to be blind or silent. Hero-worship in itself is not a preventive of a balanced biography. James Boswell was a hero-worshipper, but his devotion to Johnson did not keep him from making a realistic masterpiece. Great American biographies have been written by men who felt a deep reverence for their heroes. These books, however, were written in the spirit of the terms which Johnson himself had laid down: "If we owe regard to the memory of the dead, there is yet more respect to be paid to Knowledge, to virtue and to truth."

Hero-worship is an abiding part of the emotional life of a nation. Every generation feels that adoration, although the type of hero on whom it is bestowed, and the manner in which it is paid, are determined by the events and conditions in each generation. The biographers, like other Americans of the early nineteenth century, regarded the builders of the Republic with mingled gratitude and reverence and sentiment. In that frame of mind they could follow wholeheartedly the time-honored dictum that only good should be said of the dead. The biographers knew that their heroes had had human frailties, but in their minds the deeds of the patriots and statesmen eclipsed personal shortcomings. Why speak of faults when proven virtues were so strong? In making their portraits and narratives, the authors were governed by their sympathies as well as by biographic custom. The virtues of the great were emphasized, and the faults were forgotten or at least were not usually recounted in books. With patriotic idealism the life-writers looked up at their heroes, and like Cotton Mather and his colonial worthies, they portrayed the figures as "loyal posterity longed to believe them." The early biographers and historians thus helped to establish a national consciousness and a love of country.

"The historian of Washington is the great teacher of the nation, who tells us what sacrifices it cost our fathers to prepare for us the blessings that we enjoy; what heroism was required to overcome the obstacles that beset their path; what self-denial it demanded to forget themselves in their love for posterity; how strong their wills, how firm their hearts, how sound their judgment, how serene their wisdom."[5]

The practice of indiscriminate eulogy did not flourish unchallenged. An anonymous critic raised a voice against the custom in 1799: "To think and speak well of the distinguished dead is pleasant to the benevolent mind; and to do so to an excessive degree may be oftentimes an amiable fault: but the biographer owes it to truth and his fellow men, to paint without flattery or concealment; to present virtues, wherever he finds them, in the glory of their native colouring; and the shades of imperfection and vice, which may be discovered, without reserve or softening."[6]

In writing of biographical portraiture in the early part of the nineteenth century, Robert Walsh, an editor of Philadelphia, said that "your modern biographer. . .never places before you the poor reasonable animal, as naked as nature made him; but represents him uniformly as a demi-god."[7]

---

[5]Review of Washington Irving's life of Washington in the *North American Review*, Vol. LXXXVI, p. 357, April 1858.

[6]*Monthly Magazine and American Review*, Vol. I, p. 287, July 1799.

[7]*American Quarterly Review*, Vol. I, p. 2, March 1827.

In the adolescent stage of the nation the feeling of patriotism and the sense of national pride were not yet tempered
by the trials of experience and the realities of self-criticism.
These two things would have toned down the extravagant
strain in life-writing. Certain biographers of the twentieth
century, who have attempted to depict the complete man
rather than simply to celebrate characters and deeds, have
done a needed service in correcting and enlarging the early
portraits. The later studies, however, have not changed the
essential nature of the founders and their achievements.

III

Some objections to the laudatory lives of the early nineteenth century were based on artistic grounds. Other head-
shaking was caused by partisan prejudice or personal an-
imosity. Staunch party men read biographies as they read
their newspapers: to confirm their political faiths or to gratify their private convictions. An extreme Federalist would
abhor a eulogistic life of Jefferson; a radical Republican
would deny that a favorable political account of Washington
could truthfully be written. Strong partisans wanted biographies that backed up their own judgments of public men.
This attitude explains in part some of the encomiastic lives
of the time. There were authors on the opposite side who
attempted to prove that this man or that was an over-rated
nonetity, a demagogue, or the devil incarnate. Some of the
writers of this school were temperate in their detraction;
others abused their victims with all the invectives at their
command. The number of biographies of this kind was small
in the first half of the century.

Jefferson was early the victim of a work of slander, which
was not biography but a political tract. It bore the innocent-

sounding title, *Memoirs of the Honorable Thomas Jefferson*. It was published in 1809, the year in which Jefferson completed his second term as president. The contents of the "memoirs" were far from being innocent in language and intent. The book, which was in two volumes, was a concoction of malicious propaganda in which a part of Jefferson's life was interwoven with historical happenings in a manner to defame him and his administration. The work contained alleged instances of Jefferson's hypocrisy in his public acts, his alliance with the Jacobins, his hostility to religion, and the complete failure of his administration. The author was a Federalist writer, Stephen C. Carpenter, but his name, as well as that of the publisher, was omitted from the title page. The book was considered to be too abusive even in an age which knew no quarter in political fights, and it was suppressed close upon its publication. An unknown number of copies got into circulation.

The first American biography of Thomas Paine was an inevitable sequel to a career that had closed in a tempest of defamation and abuse. It was a malicious volume written from the motives of enmity and revenge. The author was James Cheetham, editor of a political organ in New York, once a hero-worshipper of Paine and later a bitter enemy. Cheetham had good reason to reverse his attitude. Paine had discovered that the editor "was betraying the Jeffersonian party while his paper was enjoying its official patronage." Paine exposed Cheetham unsparingly, and the latter replied with a burst of vituperation. As Paine was about to begin suit for libel, he died. Cheetham followed up his attack by publishing the biography (1809) soon after Paine's death. In the narrative he rehashed the old detractions of his victim and added new tales of his own invention.[8]

---

[8] Moncure D. Conway, *Life of Thomas Paine*, Preface p. xxiv.

A book of this kind about another public man would have been quickly suppressed or angrily cried down, but this life remained to become a source of other derogatory sketches and accounts. The biography did not start the tide of opinion against Paine. Long before his death he had been mercilessly denounced by opponents of his political principles and deistic beliefs, and his reputation had withered before the heat of their attacks. The book helped to strengthen the case against the dead defendant. To his enemies it was a medium of richly deserved retribution. To credulous readers it gave authority to the charges and accusations that had been flung at its figure. Long after Cheetham had been discredited as a biographer, the features of his false portrait of Paine remained in the public mind.

IV

By the close of the second decade of the century, when the nation was thirty years old, biography was being written to an extent that was noteworthy. The general quality of the product, however, was ordinary. According to contemporary testimony, there was wide interest in biographical sketches, notices and anecdotes, but the taste for life-narratives was not discriminating. Jared Sparks, biographer and historian, questioned the effect of the taste on literature. Sparks deplored two aspects of the condition: that so many biographies of persons of no visible achievement were being written, and that the authors were resorting so much to panegyric and invention.[9]

Another critic applied the term "biographical mania" to "the eagerness with which every species of biography is read in the present day." This writer commented on the manifest desire of readers to know the private lives of public men:

---

[9] *North American Review*, Vol. VI, p. 293, March 1818.

" 'The march of intellect,' so called, has rendered nearly every man of only limited acquirements a thinker and an observer, and the result of this improvement is that public characters are scanned with a minuteness or a severity unknown to our progenitors." The senator, the judge or the counsellor, the divine, the soldier, and authors and artists "must be content to withdraw from the bright halo of fame and splendor with which they are usually surrounded; and, arrayed in their 'dressing-gown and slippers,' are compelled to stand the test of the universal gaze. And is there not an advantage in thus denuding public men of all the pomp and mystery of office and situation? Most assuredly there is; more especially in a republican government, where the ruling men of the times should be known as they really are."[10]

---

[10] *The New-York Mirror,* Vol. VII, p. 359, May 15, 1830.
Biographical glimpses of private life were not new in the 1830s. John Norton, in his memoir of John Cotton, had described the manner in which the divine spent the Sabbath in his family circle. Ebenezer Turell had devoted two chapters of his memoir to the more personal side of Benjamin Colman's life. An early account of Washington informed the reader of a typical day in the home life of the former president after he had retired to Mount Vernon. (*Philadelphia Monthly Magazine,* Vol. I, p. 306, June 1789.)

CHAPTER IV

JARED SPARKS

The men and women who founded the little common-wealths of New England, wrote Moses Coit Tyler, were, from the first, a race of diarists, biographers and historians. Their children and their children's children were like them. With the passing of the generations the historic feeling thrived and grew lustier, nourishing itself on a finer and broader acceptance of life and on the memory of its own heroic age.[1]

Among the distinguished heirs of this spirit in the nine-teenth century was Jared Sparks, "the father of American history" and "the American Plutarch." The work of Sparks was so extensive that he virtually filled an alcove of his own in the pantheon of lives. He planned and carried out with collaborators the largest series of American biographies then in existence. He wrote twelve lives, and he made vast collections of the letters and papers of two foremost Americans of the Revolutionary time. He advanced biographical and historical scholarship by his method of intensive research

[1] *A History of American Literature,* Vol. II, p. 132.

and his painstaking study of original sources. He wrote book reviews and biographical criticism. He was the first professor of history in an American college, holding a chair at Harvard. Later he became president of that institution. Pioneer though he was in some respects, Sparks carefully observed the established canons of biographical writing and presented his heroes in the conventional manner of his time. Despite his assiduous search for facts, he did not depart from the path of conformity; he rather gave new support to the school of hero-worship.

The *Library of American Biography* consisted of twenty-five volumes and comprised the lives of fifty-eight men and two women. Each book contained one to four biographies. Sparks wrote eight of the accounts. The others were done by his associates, thirty-six in number, among whom were William B. O. Peabody, Alexander H. Everett, William H. Prescott, George S. Hillard and John G. Palfrey. The *Library* was published in two series of ten and fifteen volumes (1834-38, 1844-48). Sparks' tentative plan was to include eventually the lives of all persons who had been distinguished in America from the date of its first discovery to his own time. The project was never completed in that form. The sixty lives in the *Library* covered only segments of the broad historical area of the original plan.

Among the superior accounts in the series are those of John Ledyard, which was written by Sparks, Cotton Mather by Peabody, John Eliot by Convers Francis, Charles Brockden Brown by Prescott, and Nathanael Greene by George W. Greene.[2]

It is easy to find faults in the *Library*: to question the inclusion of certain names and the absence of others, to regret

---

[2]The two women included in the *Library* were Lucretia M. Davidson, poet, a memoir of whom was contributed by Catharine M. Sedgwick, and Anne Hutchinson, whose life was narrated by George E. Ellis.

the discrepancies in treatment and qualities and the deficiency in needed material, to point out flaws in character portrayal and the frequent lack of the critical spirit. The work as a whole, however, was a valuable addition to the biographical literature of the mid-century. It made available accounts of many men whose lives had not been published before. It brought together the best collection of native biographies in this country at that time.

The biographies that Sparks wrote, as well as the lives his associates contributed to the *Library*, have been superseded by the studies of later authors. Nothing, however, has displaced the great service which Sparks performed for American history. He travelled in this country and in Europe, and gathered an immense quantity of letters, papers and documents relating to the actors and events of the Revolution. This body of material, which Sparks took pains to preserve carefully, became an invaluable firsthand source to historians and biographers. Sparks made immediate use of much of the material. He published a part of the writings of Washington in twelve volumes (1834-38) and those of Franklin in ten volumes (1836-40). He wrote for the former collection a life of Washington, and he added to Franklin's *Autobiography* his own account of the last thirty years of Franklin's career which—as has been said—the latter never recorded. Sparks also published a work of three volumes on Gouverneur Morris which comprised a biography of the statesman and selections from his correspondence and other papers.

In the Advertisement with which he introduced his *Library* to the public, Sparks said:

"The two principal objects to be attained, in biographical compositions, are accuracy as to facts and finish in literary execution. The former demands research, the latter labor and skill. Biography is only another form of history; truth is the first requisite, simplicity of style the next. It admits of no embellishments that would give it the air of fiction; and yet its office is but half done, unless it mingles entertainment with instruction."

The theory thus stated is an excellent basis for the writing of biography. However Sparks may have attempted to apply it, the principles were modified in practice by his conception of a biographer's duties. When he embarked on a biography, Sparks became in effect the guardian of his hero's name and fame. To him *truth* seems to have been governed by consideration for the best interests of his figure. There was a quasi irrelevance to anything of a detractive nature, which, if it were used at all, should be toned down. The faults of reality should be corrected in the biographical record.

"Well written biographies," Sparks wrote, "have a charm which is seldom found in other types of writing. We have a natural interest in the fortunes of other persons. Above all do we like to follow the rise of a man through obstacles and adversities to a position of success and influence. There is a sacredness in the fame of such a man. We regard with reverence the name and virtues of that man, and we are ready to charge with sacrilege and brand with infamy the wretch who attempts to destroy the hallowed glory of that name. A great advantage of a biography of this kind is the encouraging example it offers to those who have yet their course to run."[3]

The life of Washington was written in the spirit of this viewpoint. With his skill as a biographer and the abundance of official papers in his possession, Sparks was able to com-

---

[3]Review of *Sketches of the Life and Character of Patrick Henry, North American Review,* Vol. VI, p. 293, March 1818.

pose an excellent formal biography of his hero. Although
some of the papers showed that Washington had been a man
of real human sensibilities, the portrait as Sparks drew it
had few signs of these traits. A biography written for the
public was not a book for personal and private details,
which, after all, it seemed to him, were not essential to the
picture. The life by Sparks was far superior to the work by
John Marshall in scholarship and composition.

Sparks believed that Washington's letters in their published form should be in keeping with the exalted position
of the man. Out of respect to the writer he altered and
bowdlerized the papers to conform to his conception of the
president's public reputation. Washington had once written: "$100,000 will be but a flea-bite to our demands." The
word "flea-bite" was changed to "totally inadequate." In a
sentence in which Washington had spoken of "our rascally
privateersmen" the expressive adjective was omitted. Washington's reference to "Old Put" was made to read "General
Putnam." Sparks made a vast number of changes and dele-
tions in the papers. Collectively they amounted to a great
variation from Washington's own statements. The writings
by Franklin were subjected to the same treatment. In
neither work did Sparks indicate the alterations and omissions he had made.

When his manner of editing was discovered, he was both
criticised and supported in the small tempest which ensued.
He was defended on the ground that Washington had begun
to revise his letters before he died and that the biographer
had only completed the revision. Sparks argued that it
would be an act of unpardonable injustice to any author
to publish, without the necessary revision, letters which had
been written without intention of publication. He had, it
was said, only carried out an agreement he had made with

Bushrod Washington and John Marshall. Then, too, Sparks followed a frequent though not universal practice of the time in which changes in original documents were not always made clear and quotation marks were loosely used. The controversy had the beneficial result of establishing a standard of literal accuracy for future scholars.[4]

---

[4]To what extent this rule may have been broken by editors of letters and diaries since that time is a matter of conjecture. Undoubtedly some have believed, like Jared Sparks, that private papers could be revised for publication. The changes which Sparks made in Washington's letters came to light because the original papers were available for inspection and could be compared with the published versions. If the originals of all letters and diaries were likewise open to examination, similar discrepancies and omissions might be discovered in some cases.

CHAPTER V

WASHINGTON IRVING

Washington Irving wrote biography intermittently throughout his literary career. His chief works in this field were the lives of Columbus, Oliver Goldsmith and Washington. These books held a distinguished place among biographies of the nineteenth century. They still retain some of their original value, but later generations have turned more often to their own interpretations of the men Irving portrayed.

The life of Columbus was the outcome of a proposal made to him by Alexander H. Everett, then American minister to Spain. At Everett's suggestion Irving, who was in France at the time, went to Madrid to look into the possibility of making for American readers an English translation of a collection of documents relating to the voyages of Columbus. The collection was the work of Don Martin Fernandez de Navarrete, secretary of the Royal Academy of History. Struck by the richness of the material in the collection, Irving decided to write a history of the life and voyages of the explorer.

In executing this plan, he was essentially the romanticist he had been in *The Sketch Book*. When he turned biographer, he added some of the trappings of the historical novel. He depicted "the magnificent dreamer" in an imaginative manner, adorning his narrative with picturesque incidents and descriptions, heightening the story of the voyages with dramatic effects, and imbuing the history with the sentiment that was characteristic of him. Irving gave no philosophical treatment or critical judgment to his material. His method was that of an imaginative artist employing effectively the resources of his art on a fascinating subject. Embellished as the biography was, it did not lack the virtue of painstaking preparation. Behind the drama of Irving's pages were many months of hard work and honest effort. *The Life and Voyages of Christopher Columbus* was published in three volumes in 1828.

In re-creating his hero by the romantic process, Irving differed from those of his contemporaries who depicted their figures in the formal manner. He was similar to them in obeying the canon of *nil nisi bonum*. Like other biographers he made the familiar avowal of fidelity to his subject. He recognized that human nature is a composite of conflicting elements. In discussing the character of Columbus at the end of the book, he said:

"He who paints a great man merely in great and heroic traits, though he may produce a fine picture, will never present a faithful portrait. Great men are compounds of great and little qualities. Indeed, much of their greatness arises from their mastery over the imperfections of their nature, and their noblest actions are sometimes struck forth by the collisions of their merits and their defects. (Book XVIII, Ch. V.)

In actual practice Irving made little use of the principle

he stated here. He leaned instead toward the view he expressed in an earlier part of the book:

"There is a certain meddlesome spirit, which, in the garb
of learned research, goes prying about the traces of history,
casting down its monuments, and marring and mutilating
its fairest trophies. Care should be taken to vindicate great
names from such pernicious erudition. It defeats one of the
most salutary purposes of history, that of furnishing examples of what human genius and laudable enterprise may
accomplish." (Book I, Ch. VI.)

Here Irving shows a kinship with Cotton Mather and
Jared Sparks. He would be no iconoclast. A venerated name
should not be tampered with by scholarly investigation. Let
the great remain free from critical reappraisal. According
to this standpoint, the new findings of research could not be
adopted unless they conformed to orthodox opinion or
strengthened an established fame. Learning which discovers
flaws in a nation's heroes is destructive. As a result history
becomes mythology.

In the life of Goldsmith (1849) Irving portrayed the
engaging personality which revealed itself in the pages of
The Vicar of Wakefield. Temperamentally Irving was fully
at home with Goldsmith. His spiritual and literary kinship
with the creator of Dr. Primrose has been exaggerated, but
there was unquestionably a resemblance between the two
men. The biographical sympathy which Irving felt for his
subject is pronounced. He tinted his style to harmonize with
the character of Goldsmith, and he depicted his hero in a
sentimental tone and with a romantic charm.

Irving did little or no original research in preparing the
life. He depended on the work of earlier scholars, and he
did not always use the latest material. Irving made one inexcusable digression in the biography by crossing the line

of sheer invention. He took from the biographer John For-
ster a mere possibility regarding the friendship of Goldsmith
and Mary Horneck, the "Jessamy Bride," and elaborated
the idea into a full-blown love episode for which there was
meager evidence. Being widely read in the nineteenth century, the biography established the popular conception of
Goldsmith with the baseless legend.

Irving closed his career with the life of Washington in
five volumes (1855-59). He had long desired to write a
biography of the man, and he undertook the work as a labor
of love. Irving had been born in the generation of infant
Washingtons, and he felt the attachment of a namesake for
his subject. The biography was written in a different fashion
from the lives of Columbus and Goldsmith. Although it
bore marks of the earlier Irving, notably in its imaginative
strain, it lacked the strongly romantic and sentimental treatment with which he had portrayed the other figures. The
chronicle was a reconstruction of Washington's life without
undue embellishment from the biographer. Irving interwove
the personal account of his hero with the history of the time
without allowing men and events to obscure the central
figure. The battles of the Revolution, the party struggles,
and the sketches of the military and political figures became
logical segments of the chronicle. The better parts of the
biography are those which unfold Washington's career and
depict his qualities as a man, a military leader and a
statesman.

Irving's work was unlike earlier biographies of Washington. The story by Parson Weems had been effusive, didactic
and fictional. The official life by John Marshall had been
more historical and less enlightening of its subject. That by
Jared Sparks, to whom Irving was greatly indebted, was
formal, more imposing and more scholarly. Irving observed

on the whole the traditional concept of his hero and wrote with a venerating pen. At the same time he put a new animation into his chronicle, and he invested his figure with a humanness that had not appeared in previous biographies of Washington.

The life received a cordial reception in many quarters. It was, a critic commented, "a biography essentially popular, fitted to interest young and old, erudite and ignorant." The work became a standard life of Washington, and it held a high place in biographical literature for the next thirty years. It was "the first great American biography" (Allan Nevins). Like its contemporary lives of other great men, the work has been superseded in the twentieth century.

Chapter VI

CRITICISM AND INVENTORY AT THE MID-NINETEENTH CENTURY

The attitude which Jared Sparks took toward his characters was shared by many other biographers in the middle years of the century. This viewpoint was tempered by an adherence to the existing proprieties. Always responsive to the contemporary spirit, biography was peculiarly susceptible to the code which was ascendant in those years. Authors who inherited the precept that they should speak only good of their subjects easily adopted this standard of decorum. The old commandment was invested with new authority. Convention bade the biographer to be restrained and demanded in his work the marks of refinement, dignity and good breeding. A judicious observance of these qualities would have done no harm. The fault lay in their being heeded excessively and accentuated at the expense of the figures under portrayal. Life-records were carefully distilled, and life-accounts were written to conform to the amenities of polite circles. Gentlemen were depicted as it was proper for the immediate public and posterity to know them. As a result they lost some of the human qualities and the natural manner they had had in real life. The age put its stamp of approval on "correct" portraits. This code actively regulated biographical practice in the eastern and southern parts of the country until the 1870s.

A representative biography which met exactly the standards of the mid-century was *Memoirs of William Wirt* (1849), which was written by John P. Kennedy, a romantic novelist of Maryland and Virginia. The memoirs contain a full and probably accurate account of Wirt's career. The portrait is that of a genial gentleman of the old school whose character, manners and deportment are refined of any imperfections by an affectionate and revering friend. Kennedy defended his portrayal of his subject with an argument that would have been maintained by innumerable biographers of the period.

"I hold it to be the biographer's duty," he wrote, "to turn the virtues of an illustrious man to the best account, by giving them a prominence which shall conciliate all regard. The faults of a good man are but transient blemishes, which quickly fade from view. His virtues are unchangeable, ever present and imperishable. He who has to speak of both should observe the proportion indicated by this truth."

Decorous and discreet as the biographies of the mid-century seem today, the feeling existed among some persons that they made unwarranted disclosures of the private affairs of their figures. It was not that the biographers exposed family skeletons or spread scandal in their pages—offenses which they clearly did not commit. Their transgression lay in crossing the line of a man's public career into his private life. This view was voiced by Andrew P. Peabody, editor of the *North American Review*. He declared that "the greater portion of recent biographical literature" was guilty of this breach of propriety and played "a traitor's part with the well-earned reputation of their subjects." Dr. Peabody argued that "no man would willingly live in a house of glass. Why should the walls of a great man's dwelling be made transparent as soon as he is translated from it? The portions of the life that are by the common instinct kept from day to day sacred from the public gaze, should remain inviolate."

Dr. Peabody also charged the biographies of the time with two great defects: their lack of proportion and their excessive length. He complained of "these memoirs of massive volumes; these prolix chapters devoted to the details of pedigree, the pranks and follies and whippings of childhood, the minutiae of courtship and of housekeeping; these masses of trivial correspondence; these sweepings of desks and commonplace books." Biographies of this kind, he said, would, because of their length and trivia, remain unread by future generations. He called for biographers who would follow the example of Plutarch in his "commendable brevity, and confine themselves to the salient traits, the characteristic acts, and the public relations of his heroes." Answering the assertion that "these prolix biographies" would be storehouses of information for the future historian, Dr. Peabody declared that "they are rather rendering the labors of that mythical personage impossible, unless he shall be a Hercules in his working force, and a Methuselah in the years allotted for his life-task."[1]

Another critic took the position that the full truth should be told for its instructive value. In discussing the duty of a biographer, this writer said that a man's life "is a lesson to mankind, and futurity may play over the game which he lived; see where the mismove was made, and learning by his experience, shun similar errors in their own conduct.

[1] *North American Review*, Vol. LXXXIX, p. 521, October 1859.

The author has not, therefore, a moral right from any partiality to the subject of his biography, either to conceal the deviations, or to put a false gloss upon the faults of one who belongs to the world's history . . . . The oft-repeated 'de mortuis nil, nisi bonum' has not only been the cause, or the apology, for very great falsehood, but has also done a vast amount of injury . . . . By speaking of a man's good qualities, and few have none, in a becoming manner, and omitting all mention of his faults, a good reputation is easily acquired. Biography becomes *eulogium*, and its great end, truth, is not only lost, but falsehood is propagated . . . . There is a duty we owe to the living which far outstrips that which we owe to the dead." The duty is summed up in the motto, *de mortuis nil, nisi verum*.[2]

A third critic of the mid-century, Evert A. Duyckinck, pointed out the harm done by unqualified and irresponsible writers who adopt the guise of biographers and turn out lives with little concern for the laws and obligations of the craft.

"It certainly appears," Duyckinck wrote, "that biography, as an art, defined in its range and exhibitions by critical and moral laws, has received far less attention from the world than the importance of the subject demands. In our own day, particularly, when there are more 'Lives' written in proportion to the bulk of literature than ever before, there is less deference to rule, and apparently less sense of responsibility, in their preparation than ever before. Every man fortunate or unhappy enough to come into possession of a trunk full of papers relating to some departed man or woman of eminence,—nor is it always necessary that the man or woman should have departed this life, or that the eminence be unquestionable,—thinks himself *ipso facto* qualified to set up as a biographer. . . . Genius, talent, high position, are in hourly danger, and alas for the literature of the nineteenth century and the burdens we are imposing upon posterity! low life, mediocrity, dulness itself,—these afford no protection from the biographical assassins swarming in all directions."[3]

Before Duyckinck sounded this blast, another reviewer had in 1850 voiced alarm over the quantity of biographical volumes that was being loaded on the bookshelves. The shelves, he wrote, "already bend and creak under the ponderous mass of 'Lives' and 'Memoirs,' with which they are oppressed; and we begin to calculate with dismay how many tons will they have to bear in those glorious days, when, as the statisticians love to tell us, our population shall amount to a hundred millions, and our great men shall lie around us as thick as the leaves in Vallombrosa?"[4]

II

Besides writing voluminously, the biographers of the first half of the nineteenth century peopled their shelves with a wide variety of characters. Their devotion to the heroes of the Revolutionary era has been seen. The broad range which American life-literature had reached by the mid-century is rendered evident by biographies which are representative of other categories of figures. Among the types who were portrayed most numerously during this period were military men: Andrew Jackson (1824) by John H. Eaton, Winfield Scott (1852) by Edward D. Mansfield; naval commanders: Oliver H. Perry (1820) by John M. Niles, Stephen Decatur (1846) by Alexander S. Mackenzie; political figures: Henry Clay (1845) by Calvin Colton, John C. Calhoun (1850)

---

[3]*North American Review*, Vol. LXXXIV, p. 406, April 1857.
[4]In review of Kennedy, *Memoirs of the Life of William Wirt, North American Review*, Vol. LXX, p. 255, January 1850.

by John S. Jenkins; pioneers: Daniel Boone (1833) by Timothy Flint; travellers: John Ledyard (1828) by Jared Sparks; and criminals: John C. Colt (1842) by an anonymous writer.

Clergymen continued to be favorite subjects, and a great number of lives of contemporary ministers were written by relatives and friends. These books as a rule sprang from the tradition inherited from the Colonial time that the lives of church leaders should be preserved as a tribute to them and an example to others. The accounts tended to be eulogistic, in many cases excessively so, and they were often marred by the faults of unskilled writers. One of the most successful clerical biographies, and a work which stood apart from the inferior volumes of its class, was the life of Jonathan Edwards (1830) by Sereno E. Dwight.

During the first half of the nineteenth century the man of letters hardly appeared as a subject in biography. A life of Charles Brockden Brown, novelist and critic, and commonly called the first professional man of letters in the United States, was written by Paul Allen and William Dunlap. Brown died in 1810. This was the first biography of a professional author to be published (1815) in this country. The book is more a miniature anthology of Brown than a biography in the generally accepted sense. The narrative of his life is short, and it contains inaccuracies. The remainder of the two volumes is made up of selections from his works and his letters.

Among the remaining types which were added to biography in this period were the woman of letters: Margaret M. Davidson (1841) by Washington Irving; teacher: John Griscom (1859) by John H. Griscom; editor: Isaac Hill (1835) by Cyrus P. Bradley; physician: John C. Warren (1860) compiled by Edward Warren; surgeon: John Clement (1813) by John Hooper; humanitarian: Thomas Eddy (1834) by Samuel L. Knapp; Indian chief: Black Hawk (1838) by Benjamin Drake; Negro slave: Sojourner Truth (1850) by an anonymous biographer; and mountaineer and hunter: James C. Adams (1860) by Theodore H. Hittell.

III

For thirty years after his death in 1826 no life of Thomas Jefferson did justice to the biographical stature of the man. Several sympathetic and laudatory volumes were published during that time, but in none of these was his career set forth in the detail and length which it deserved, whether from an objective or a partisan standpoint. The adherents of Jefferson did not lack qualified biographers, the voluminous papers and documents relating to his varied achievements were available, and a great American needed a comprehensive biography. Yet no chronicle of this kind appeared until the middle of the century (1858).

It was a work in three volumes by Henry S. Randall, a native of New York state, who combined a lifelong interest in practical agriculture with a strong devotion to public education. Randall was allowed to use the papers in the possession of the Jefferson family, and he brought together in an organized form for the first time an extensive amount of authentic information concerning his subject. The book lacked judicial interpretation of its data. Randall was an ardent believer in Jefferson's political philosophy, and he composed the biography with the zeal and enthusiasm of a wholehearted partisan. He advocated Jefferson's principles with strong feeling, and he showed no tolerance for the political opponents of his hero. Randall wrote his narrative in a plain and vigorous style, but he repeatedly sinned against the common laws of grammar and composition. The biography is far from being a work of art, but with all its limitations the book remains a significant item in the bibliography of Jefferson.

CHAPTER VII

INTRODUCTION TO THE LATER NINETEENTH
CENTURY

During the twenty-five years that followed the end of the
Civil War—from 1865 to 1890—the course of life-writing
was not marked by the phenomena which appeared in other
branches of literature. No biographic Whitman sounded his
"barbaric yawp" through the pantheon of biography. No
pilot from the Mississippi River protested its portraits in
iconoclastic terms. No Pike characters from the Mid-West
or California joined the diversified company assembled in
its galleries. No counterpart of Joaquin Miller from Oregon
celebrated the pioneer heroes of the westward march. The
call for newness and realism that was answered so vigorously
in the post-war literature did not immediately penetrate the
main body of biography. The nation's awakening experience in the conflict wrought no sudden changes in biographical practice.

Yet during the twenty-five years after the war the traditional principles of life-writing were slowly subjected to the
play of two great forces. The first of these was the new spirit

of scientific inquiry which rose from the doctrines of Darwin and others of his time. The fresh interest in the Fact *per se* spurred biographers to study their subjects more deeply and dispassionately. The second factor was the vitalizing power of literary realism, a product of the scientific spirit, which enabled them to present their figures in a more lifelike manner. The action of these forces on biography was gradual in its effect and not spectacular in its results, but the influence of the forces becomes more and more perceptible in the later decades of the century.

II

Long before the tumult and the shouting of the war had ceased, the biographers were at work on the new figures who were thrown into prominence by the struggle. In the biographical sense alone, Lincoln was by far the most significant of these characters. The biographers of the war figures were more numerous in the North than in the South. The writers in both sections paid more attention to military heroes than to leaders in political affairs. Among the army men Grant, Sherman and Sheridan, and Lee and "Stonewall" Jackson were of chief interest to the biographers.

Except for the lives of Jefferson Davis, the biographies written on both sides applauded their figures and more often were lavish in their praise. The elation of victory, a loyal devotion to gallant officers, and the mental relief brought by peace thrilled the writers to eulogy and reduced their critical objectivity. Davis was both praised and blamed by Southern authors. His conduct of the war, which became highly controversial, as well as some of his personal qualities, which were thought to have contributed to the defeat of the Confederacy, made him the target of strong attacks. A biography which contains this point of view is *Life of*

Jefferson Davis, With a Secret History of the Southern Confederacy (1869), by Edward A. Pollard. The author was editor of a newspaper in Richmond.

The total output of "war lives" during the conflict and in the next twenty-five years was enormous. The careers of innumerable officers in the Northern armies were recounted by relatives and friends. The dramatic appearance of so many potential figures quickened the efforts of professional biographers and fired a host of amateur writers whose enthusiasm for their heroes greatly exceeded their knowledge and skill in the art. Except for certain lives of Lincoln, the biographies of this period which resulted from the war are seldom recalled now except by students and specialists in the field.*

Personal Memoirs of U. S. Grant (1885, 1886), which was his "last victory," has a place in the group of leading American autobiographies.

CHAPTER VIII

BIOGRAPHIES OF LINCOLN, 1860-1890

The biographical interest in Lincoln's life was originally political and transient. It sprang from the need for informative accounts which would make the Republican candidate known to the electorate during his two campaigns for the presidency. Many short biographies were hastily prepared for that purpose and rushed into print in 1860 and 1864. After each election the interest had subsided, and the campaign biographies, their usefulness ended, had been thrown aside. The death of Lincoln in 1865, only six weeks after his second inauguration, instantly changed his position in biography. The interest in the man and his life then shifted to the historic. It became permanent, widening and deepening with the years. As time went on, the biographies of Lincoln multiplied without cessation. They now form the largest number of books written about an American figure.

Lincoln possesses a transcendent appeal to biographers and biographiles alike. The character of the president and his place in history make him a figure of perpetual interest. Today he represents what Democracy has achieved in the

United States, and he is a symbol of what it strives to accomplish. As a folk hero he embodies "the qualities that we most admire or desire in ourselves." His individuality and career reflect universal experiences and ideals. The mere narrative of his life, unfolded without technical manipulation or fictional embroidery, contains within itself the elements of a historical novel and a tragic drama. The story has the substance of an epic that rises from the homely setting of the prairie years to the heroic climax in Washington.

In the nineteenth century Lincoln was seen in the inevitable different lights by different authors. This variation in viewpoint has spurred biographers of the twentieth century to attempt an all-inclusive portrait and its resultant interpretation. Lincoln's life was filled with controversial points and problematic happenings which have engrossed investigators and piqued lay persons. Even if and when the whole truth is known about the man, the line of Lincoln biographies will not end. New biographies of merit will always compel attention. The best of the older lives will still be read.

When Lincoln died, no publisher had an adequate biography to offer the public. More than ever before the people were now eager to read the story of his life. There was an obvious advantage to the publishers in putting new books on the market as soon as possible. A biography that is read in the mood of grief possesses an emotional immediacy that is lacking in later works. Secretary Stanton, standing at Lincoln's bedside, had hardly spoken the words which were to become classic, before the earliest of the post-war biographers were at work. Some of their concoctions began to appear before the official period of mourning had terminated.

The new books increased rapidly in the following months. By the close of 1865 fifteen biographies had been published in the United States and ten in Europe. The volumes issued in this country were a diverse lot. In one of them the life of Lincoln was told as if he were still living; then the reader came abruptly to an account of his death and funeral. The main part of this book had been reprinted from a campaign biography, and the publisher would lose no time to change such a trifling thing as tense. Another firm met the same problem in an opposite way. It printed an earlier booklet on the life of the president and placed an account of his death in a new preface. Time-saving devices of this kind were an exception and not the practice in 1865. Several of the other volumes were written with serious intent even if they lacked long deliberation.

The best of the earliest biographies was that published in 1866 by Josiah Gilbert Holland, an influential editor of the Springfield (Mass.) *Republican* and a popular writer of novels, poems and essays. Holland was a "people's author," and his readers ran into the hundreds of thousands. He was essentially a moralist. His desk was a pulpit from which he addressed lay sermons and counsel on living to his large clientele. His life of Lincoln conformed to the philosophy of his other literary work. It was intended to be—in his words—a "pleasant, instructive and inspiring" biography for the general public. The life was also eulogistic in its tone, and the author drew numerous lessons from his subject's career. This was the first book on Lincoln to be made from any considerable research. Holland visited the Lincoln country and gathered much of his material from persons who had known Lincoln. His portrait bore the lines of a folk hero. It was not the man as he had actually lived, but a figure refined of all imperfections and elevated to the ideal.

Like the Holland book, the biographies of the next ten years were in key with the mood of the nation. The character they described was the emancipator and savior and martyr whom the people pictured through their gratitude, love and grief. The authors reflected the popular conception of the man and rejected whatever was inconsistent with the prevailing ideas. The biographies, in turn, confirmed the convictions of the people. The story of Lincoln was also accentuated emotionally by the assassination and the disorders of the Reconstruction years. The rapidly growing image of the folk hero was enshrined in the valhalla within a decade after his death.

There were dissenters from this mode of portraiture. One of the strongest objectors was William H. Herndon, who had been Lincoln's law partner in Springfield for sixteen years. He read the memorials of the heroic school with increasing resentment. He was a hero-worshipper as well, but the object of his veneration was not the man he found in the books. He remembered Lincoln with the realistic familiarity of a long-time associate. To Herndon's way of thinking these fastidious idolaters were doing injustice to Lincoln in refining him. Why not place the real man before the people. That was the kind of biography Herndon was then getting ready. He would unmask not his beloved old friend but the fanciful fictionists.

Herndon had set out to collect every possible bit of information about Lincoln. He traveled in Kentucky and Indiana, visiting the places where the family had lived and interviewing anyone and everyone who had known the Lincolns. He questioned and requestioned their relatives, neighbors and friends, and industriously wrote down the reminiscences that he drew forth. He scoured New Salem in Illinois an Vandalia, the old state capital where Lincoln had served in the legislature. In Springfield he added to his own knowledge with statements and recollections from persons there.

Besides gathering this verbal testimony, Herndon searched records and transcribed what he needed. He "begged or copied every personal letter of Lincoln" that he could find. He carried on an extensive correspondence, and he employed men to assist him in his research. At the death of Lincoln he acquired the papers and books of the law office in Springfield.

Herndon did not publish his biography for many years. In the meantime he allowed others to use the material he had collected. Dr. Holland obtained much data from him and trimmed it to suit his purpose. Herndon declared that Holland had misused the "facts" he had given him. Holland replied to the charge with a fiery indictment of Lamon's life of Lincoln, which he thought was largely the work of Herndon. The Lamon biography was the first to embody the Herndon material in the Herndon vein.

When Lincoln rode the circuit, Ward H. Lamon was his law partner in Danville. Their professional relation extended to marked friendship. Lamon aided Lincoln in the campaign of 1860, went to Washington with him, and was appointed by the president marshal of the District of Columbia. He remained a staunch supporter of Lincoln through the vicissitudes of the war. Soon after the death of the president Lamon resigned as marshal and formed a law partnership with Jeremiah S. Black.

Lamon also entertained the idea of writing a biography of his friend. Like Herndon he was dissatisfied with the lives that were being published. He too felt that they failed to depict the man he knew and revered. He wanted to correct the erroneous conception of Lincoln. To carry out his plan he negotiated with Herndon for the use of the material in the latter's collection, and he arranged with a publishing firm in Boston to bring out the work in two volumes.

Although Lamon possessed the firsthand knowledge of his figure and had acquired the supplementary material, he lacked the ability of a biographer. He took into partnership in the project Chauncey F. Black, son of his law associate, and left to Black the actual composition of the book. Lamon made an unwise choice of a substitute. The Blacks had been opponents of the Lincoln administration, and the political prejudice of the writer cropped out in his narrative. The first volume was published (1872) in Lamon's name alone. Black's part in the book was not known immediately.

Designed as a corrective, the volume proved to be an irritant. It was challenged in its assertions and deplored for its alleged lack of propriety. Lincoln, the book said, had scoffed at religion and mimicked preachers. "His engagement to Miss Todd was one of the great misfortunes of his life and of hers." To Lincoln men in the 1870s certain passages in the book had an inimical sound, which may be laid to Black's antipathy to his subject. Despite the maladjusted focus, the unsympathetic note, and the matter which some readers found objectionable, Lincoln appeared in this book in homely reality. The Black work was the first "analytical and critical" life of Lincoln. Though it failed of general acceptance, it was a valuable addition to the Lincoln biographies. It made available a part of the Herndon collection, and it furnished promising leads to later investigators. This first volume excited so much opposition that the second was never issued.

The adverse reception of the Lamon book was only a flurry in comparison with the storm of controversy which raged around Herndon's biography. This work, which was entitled *Herndon's Lincoln: The True Story of a Great*

Life, was published in three volumes seventeen years later, in 1889. Herndon was assisted by Jesse W. Weik, a newspaper man of Indiana, and the title-page bore both their names.

Herndon built the biography on the theory that he should give "all the facts" about his hero. In practice this principle meant to Herndon the inclusion not only of real and incontestable facts but also dubious testimony, unreliable reminiscences and sheer hearsay. He did not test his witnesses for their qualifications or weigh his evidence for its validity. He did not discriminate between the authentic and the doubtful or false. From this heterogeneous mass of material, he believed, people of his time and in the future could draw their own conclusions and form their own portrait of the hero. The possibility that an erroneous if sympathetic picture could be drawn from a mixture of fact, fancy and falsehood apparently did not concern Herndon. Whatever else his biography might yield, he took care that his case *for* Lincoln should be well-grounded and impressive. He wanted to show that his hero had risen to great heights from a lowly beginning. This motive throws much light on the nature of the chronicle.

Herndon was no objective biographer. He revelled in interpreting his data and embellishing the facts. He felt that from his experience and his knowledge of Lincoln he could understand the meaning and significance of his material. These qualifications, however, could not alter his dislikes or curb his imagination or rectify his technical principles. Herndon was both speculative and inventive. He had strong faith in his power of intuition. He poured over his material, drawing inferences and making deductions. He used his imagination freely, enlarging incidents and episodes with colorful details, and filling in gaps with fabrications of romantic texture.

The attacks on the biography were directed chiefly at certain assertions which Herndon made. He said that Lincoln had told him that Nancy Hanks, Lincoln's mother, had been an illegitimate child. Herndon was positive that the death of Ann Rutledge had affected Lincoln for the rest of his life, and the biographer gave the episode of Lincoln and Ann a far-reaching consequence which Lincoln scholars hold it never had. Herndon declared that Lincoln had purposely failed to appear at his wedding—the original ceremony which was set for January 1, 1841,—and he dwelt on the alleged unhappy marriage to Mary Todd. Herndon's treatment of Lincoln's religion brought on a debate that continued for years. The biographer quoted testimony from persons to the effect that Lincoln was unorthodox in his beliefs and "held opinions utterly at variance with what are taught by the Church."[1]

The great lack of the biography is an adequate treatment of Lincoln from 1861 to 1865. Herndon was not writing a history of the "times" of his hero, yet the barest narrative of the president during the war years deserved more than the short part which the book contains. Those were the years which gave biographical importance to the prairie years.

The biography is strong in its vitality and style. The two authors brought Lincoln to life in their book with the skill of a realistic novelist. The reader sees and feels "the presence of a living man." Herndon and Weik produced a biography of literary excellence and marked readability. The narrative is concrete and vivid. The style of the work, which is nearer the homespun than the broadcloth, fits the central figure and the story.

[1]For a summary of the recent findings by Lincoln scholars pertaining to the charges that were made against Herndon's biography, see David Donald, *Lincoln's Herndon* (1948), pp. 357-359.

Less can be said for the truth of the biography. The Herndon-Weik re-creation of Lincoln's character and life was partly true and partly false. Herndon's imaginative flights and his sheer fabrications were as unwarranted in the 1880s as they would be today. The people in his time had no way of separating the fact from the fiction, and present-day readers must consult a corrective analysis of the biography to ascertain its factual accuracy. Herndon was most dependable when he wrote from firsthand knowledge. If in its "broad outlines" of Lincoln's character and the "general substance" of its contents the biography is true, that circumstances does not lessen the valid objections which may be made to its embellishments, groundless assertions and factual errors.

The contents of the book, circulated and repeated by episodes and in anecdotes, have contributed heavily to the folk status of Lincoln. By his practice of including fancy and fiction with fact, Herndon helped to create both a realistic and a mythological Lincoln. In trying to rescue his friend from eulogy and hagiography, Herndon pointed the way to the conception of an ideal Lincoln that is a blend of myth and truth.

Two other biographers of Lincoln, John G. Nicolay and John Hay, had the great fortune to be officially and intimately associated with their subject during his years in the White House. They had known him in Springfield, and after his election they had gone to Washington to be his senior and junior secretaries. In 1861 Nicolay was twenty-nine years old, Hay was twenty-three. They were in Lincoln's service until his death. The young men were in the center of affairs around which raged the crisis of the nation's existence. "We were," they wrote, "the daily and nightly witnesses of the incidents, the anxieties, the fears, and the

hopes which pervaded the Executive Mansion and the National Capital." They early had in mind a history of Lincoln and his administration—a plan which was sanctioned
by the president,—and they began to collect material for
that purpose. After the war they added to these memorabilia from a vast mass of documents, manuscripts and books.
They labored on the composition of their work from approximately 1875 to 1885. It was published in book form in
1890.

Abraham Lincoln: A History is a work which blends
biography and history. The authors devoted ten large volumes to their undertaking. The immediate foregrounds in
which Lincoln lived, and the larger state and national backgrounds, with the men who were connected with him, are
drawn at length, and through this minute record is woven
the narrative of Lincoln's life. Nicolay and Hay portrayed
their figure in a formal, official manner as a personage before the public. They ignored certain controversial questions
and did not attempt to adjudicate points at issue. They did
not exercise the authority which was theirs to determine the
truth or falsity of earlier statements made about their subject. As Republicans who were "Lincoln men all through,"
they treated his political opponents unfavorably. They enjoyed the privilege of using papers in the possession of Lincoln's son Robert—a permission no other biographers received while the son was alive, — with the condition that
they submit their manuscript for his approval before it was
published. The great value of the Nicolay and Hay work
has been in its wealth of organized information.

The groundwork of Lincoln biography ended with this set
of volumes. In the next fifty years the library of Lincoln
books was to grow impressively from the fresh researches
and penetrating studies of numerous biographers. Besides

the formal biographies, Lincoln's life and character were to be narrated and portrayed in fiction, poetry and the drama, and an autobiographical volume was eventually composed for him.*

---

*For much of the material used in this chapter I am indebted to the following authors and their articles or books:

Paul M. Angle. Editor's Preface in Herndon's *Life of Lincoln* (World Publishing Company, reprinted 1942).

William E. Barton. "A Bibliography of Biographies of Abraham Lincoln" in *Transactions of the Illinois State Historical Society* for 1929 (Illinois State Historical Library).

David Donald. *Lincoln's Herndon* (Alfred A. Knopf, 1948).

Benjamin P. Thomas. *Portrait for Posterity* (Rutgers University Press, 1947).

CHAPTER IX

JAMES PARTON

It is in keeping with the strongly marked Americanism of James Parton to introduce him in a characteristic American manner — with superlatives and statistics. Parton was the most prolific, the most popular and the best-paid author of biography in the latter half of the nineteenth century. Within the space of thirty-one years—from 1855 to 1886—he composed the lives of six American characters and one French figure, and he compiled several volumes of collective shorter accounts.

Parton "wrote at once for the people." He carried biography directly to that vast body of mixed tastes and minds, the general public, and he was immediately accepted by the clientele he sought to have. A reviewer of the *Atlantic Monthly* in 1867 spoke in praise of the service Parton performed for the people: "The favor done to this age and generation by Mr. Parton in taking eminent public men out of the keeping of panegyric and abuse, and giving them to popular knowledge in some appreciable human quality, is scarcely to be over-estimated." (Vol. XIX, p. 636) Parton made his books highly palatable. He entertained while he enlightened. He taught while he held the interest. Yet he did not gratify his readers by flattering their prejudices, nor did he titillate them by being smart, satiric or iconoclastic. If Parton did not exemplify life-writing in its highest form, he did not impair the art or break faith with his heroes. Although he departed from biographic custom in some respects, he remained in harmony with the temper of his time. "What gives to his work its most striking originality," Charles Eliot Norton wrote in the *North American Review* in 1867, "is the fact that it is so genuine and characteristic a representation of the prevailing mental and moral conditions of the nation. Mr. Parton is the product of his age and of his country. He is strictly an American author." (Vol. 104, p. 597).

Parton was not a native of the United States. He was born in England in 1822 and was brought to this country in childhood. When a young man he engaged in journalism in New York and became a regular contributor to two popular magazines, the *Home Journal* and the *Youth's Companion*. Parton began his career of biographical authorship somewhat by chance, at the age of thirty-three. He remarked one day in the hearing of two members of a publishing firm that Horace Greeley was an excellent subject for a biography. He was soon commissioned to write the life. Greeley was then editor of the New York *Tribune*, which he had founded in 1841. A hero of the homespun type, Greeley had risen from poverty and obscurity to national fame and influence. He was a worker for reform on many fronts and an aggressive spokesman for the common man of his time. Endowed with practical common sense, high ideals and a passion for human brotherhood, Greeley was a champion of a better order of living for the plain people.

Whatever motive led Parton to mention the biography, it is logical to infer that he was actually drawn to the personality and principles of the man and was not prompted simply by the prospect of a salable book. Parton himself came to show a sympathy with such principles, and some of the figures he chose in later years for his long biographies had a kinship with the editor of the *Tribune* in their social and political philosophies. At any rate, the life of Greeley (1855) did not bear the marks of a hack product. Although it does not rank with Parton's best biographies, the book was a work of much research and skillful writing. It met with a literary success and financial profit which quickly determined Parton's future career.

His second biography was the *Life and Times of Aaron Burr* (1858). Then, as now, Burr was a controversial figure, and the odds were heavily against him in the public mind. His friend Matthew L. Davis had pictured him as a persecuted hero in an earlier life (1836, 1837), but this biography did not alter the general opinion of Burr. For years after his death in 1836 he was looked upon as "the negation of every virtue and a very fiend incarnate." His name was linked with that of Benedict Arnold as a symbol of treason and wickedness. Parton did not accept this extreme judgment of Burr. To his mind Burr's character and deeds were enveloped in a myth of distortion and falsehood. He did not have any illusion that Burr had been a wholly innocent and upright man, but he did believe that Burr's character had not been as black as it was commonly imagined. Ignoring Burr's assertion that he hated apologies and explanations. Parton set out to ascertain the true nature of his subject and to dispel the myth.

He studied his figure in the source material of the period, and he arrived at the conclusion that the evidence did not support some of the worst charges which had hitherto been unquestioned. Parton did not attempt to exonerate Burr of all the counts in the indictment, but he cited "instances of honorable sentiment, kindness and generosity" of his figure, and he exhibited "the brilliant and attractive qualities of a gifted, unprincipled and wretched man." The villain of a drama was also portrayed with attributes of a hero. To many readers this not only denied the verdict of history, but it was also an inexcusable breach in the meaning of morality.

More important, however, is the question of the soundness of Parton's interpretation. Up to the present time the answer has not been settled. As later writers have shown, it is not easy to write objectively of Aaron Burr. If Parton hoped to keep to a middle course in his interpretation, the effect of his biography, a friendly critic pointed out, was that of an "ingenious, ably argued, and manifestly sincere counter-plea" to the prosecution.[1]

In the latter part of his life Parton wrote: "I have generally had the great advantage of loving my subjects warmly; and I do not believe we can do justice to any human creature unless we love him." The fruits of this advantage, when it is reinforced by painstaking research, insight into character and events, and skillful composition, are evident in his biographies of Andrew Jackson (1860), Benjamin Franklin (1864) and Thomas Jefferson (1874). Parton admired these men and their achievements, and he was in strong sympathy with their benevolent principles. He could throw himself wholeheartedly into the task of writing their lives. He said that one of his rules of biography was "to avoid eulogy and apology and let the facts have their natural weight." In these books he did not suppress the faults of his heroes or over-estimate their virtues. As the sympathetic

---

[1]*North American Review*, Vol. LXXXVI, p. 295, January 1858.

weigh-master of his data, he read the scales in terms that
were favorable to his figures. The chronicles of these men
are all long. The history of Jefferson's life filled three volumes, the biography of Franklin was in two volumes, and
the work on Jackson ran to some seven hundred pages. They
were the most instructive and entertaining biographies of
their subjects which had been published. More scholarly
lives of Jackson, Franklin and Jefferson have since been
written, and later authors have used material which Parton
did not have, but his biographies have not lost their value.

Parton's last long biography was the *Life of Voltaire*
(1881). This work was the culmination of some twenty
years of intermittent research and study which he carried
on in secondary sources in this country. No extensive biography of Voltaire had been published by an American
author before this time. Parton wanted to exhibit to the
American people the figure whom he called in his preface
"the most extraordinary of Frenchmen, and one of the most
extraordinary of human beings." Fervid as this introductory
characterization was, it was not the keynote of the body of
the book. In the biography proper Parton was more temperate and judicial, and he did not allow his intense admiration of his hero to kindle an extravagant panegyric. Parton
was too honest a biographer and too faithful to his art not
to present Voltaire's follies and vices together with the endowments of the man. That Voltaire was the embodiment
of many men—good and bad—Parton makes clear to the
reader. The effect of the biography is that of a plea and a
defence. The two volumes which comprise the work contain
an immense amount of information about Voltaire and his
age. American readers did not respond to the biography as
eagerly as they had received the lives of Jackson, Franklin

and Jefferson. They showed a strong preference for the heroes in whom they could feel a native interest.[2]

Parton's special gift in composing his long biographies was to re-create the lives of his figures with verisimilitude. He had an exceptional skill in writing narrative, and his style was clear, direct, and often lively. "A human character is complicated," he said. "It is often inconsistent with itself, and it requires nice judgment to proportion it in such a way as to make the book really correspond with the man, and make the same impression upon the reader that the man did upon those who knew him best." This agreement with the original and the reproduction, and the same likeness of impression, Parton achieved to a high degree. The semblance to reality was basically sound. Parton built it on the factual record—as he interpreted the data. He did not make it a fictional invention in the manner of a novelist. Without formality or presumption he took his readers into the presence of his heroes and created the feeling of familiar reality.

This being the impression Parton's biographies made, what of his equipment and workmanship?

Parton's works were not flawless transcripts of the original lives. He made errors in facts, and his interpretation had the debatable judgments that are almost inevitable in the work of subjective biographers. Parton said that one of the charms of biography lay in the truth being told charitably. This principle is especially apparent in his treatment of the faults of the men whom he admired. Instead of suppressing the defects, he acknowledged them. He was inclined to present them in a manner which was so lenient or charitable that

---

[2]Among Parton's books of collective biography were: *Famous Americans of Recent Times* (1867), *People's Book of Biography* (1868), *Short Lives of the Most Prominent Persons of All Ages and Countries* (1881), *Noted Women of Europe and America* (1883), *Captains of Industry* (two series, 1884, 1891), *Some Noted Princes, Authors and Statesmen of Our Time* (1885), *Sketches of Men of Progress* (1870, 1871).

the reader often felt a similar tolerance toward the weaknesses. Parton was censured for "loose thinking and loose writing," two lapses of which were the "unconsidered assertion" and the "overcharged statement." His style was at times colloquial and careless. He was vivid and pictorial, but not poetic or philosophic. He did not have the background that is formed by broad study, long deliberation and intellectual discipline. Parton had the intuition which is needed to understand the problems of character and the implication of events. He was well versed in the biographic process. He was tireless in searching out material. He was an absorbing storyteller. His work had the virtues and the imperfections of the national culture in which he was bred.

Parton was a precursor of the biography of the twentieth century. He can not be classed wholly either with the writers of the "new" school or with the less revolutionary biographers who made marked changes in the traditional methods. Parton foreshadowed the former group in his frequent "disregard of formality and conventionalism," in his eye for effect, in his lively style, and in the feeling of familiar reality which he imparted to the reader. In his best lives, however, he showed a pains in research and a fidelity to his heroes which was not generally evident in the work of the writers of the new school. He also revealed a humane spirit which was absent from their books. Unlike them, too, he was not, as been said, satiric or iconoclastic. Parton's kinship is stronger with those later biographers who combined the best elements of the new manner with the best of the old methods.*

---

*For a book-length study of Parton's life and work, see Milton E. Flower, *James Parton: The Father of Modern Biography* (1951). The foregoing chapter was written before Mr. Flower's book was published.

Chapter X

MEN OF LETTERS AND STATESMEN

Biographic custom long decreed that in the ordinary course of affairs the life of an individual should not be published before his death. In the case of men of letters there was no reason to alter the custom. Professional authors did not run for high office, they did not lead armies or win military battles, nor did they turn rogues or criminals,—three conditions which would have made them qualified to receive biographical attention while they were living. Although sketches and critical essays of authors were published, literary figures had as a rule ended their careers before they were considered to be appropriate subjects for extended biographies.[1]

Before these were compiled, the men of letters, like persons in other fields, were commemorated in obituaries and memorial addresses and were recalled in the frag-

---

[1] A life of John Greenleaf Whittier by William S. Kennedy, published in 1882, when the poet was at the height of his fame, and ten years before his death, was criticised by one reviewer as being "premature." But a study of Emerson's life and work by George W. Cooke, published in the year before Emerson died, had favorable acceptance.

mentary memoirs and reminiscent accounts of their friends and associates.

Of the men who are now regarded as the major authors of the century, Poe was the first to die. For years following his death in 1849 his life-record was clouded in mystery and controversy. Numerous articles were written in the as-I-knew-him vein in attempts to establish the truth about the poet's character and career. In 1880, thirty years after his death, John H. Ingram, an Englishman, published in London a life of Poe in two volumes. Although this work was not wholly accurate or complete, it was the first extended study to picture Poe in something like a true light. The book went through several editions in England and the United States.

In 1885 George E. Woodberry wrote a life of Poe for the American Men of Letters Series which had been recently inaugurated. This biography was far superior in its contents and workmanship to that by Ingram. Woodberry later (1909) revised and expanded the original book in an independent work of two volumes. In their general plan and contents the two editions may properly be considered together. Woodberry's purpose was to combine an interpretative narrative of Poe's life with a critical examination of his writings. The biographer applied to the task the talents of a masterly craftsman and a fair and discriminating critic. He treated his figure's career in a candid and sympathetic manner, and he analyzed Poe's work in poetry, the short story and criticism with sound judgment. The biographer's two strands of narrative and criticism were skillfully knitted together to form a proportioned and logical whole. Woodberry's second book on Poe is a model of the type of critical biography.

Washington Irving provided for his own biography. He

knew that a life would be written by someone, and he made
his nephew, Pierre M. Irving, his executor, entrusting to the
younger man his diaries, letters and other papers. The official family chronicle, which took the form of the life-and-
letters type, was published in four volumes (1862-64) soon
after Irving's death in 1859. The work was a conventional
narrative composed in the manner of the mid-century. By
making liberal use of letters and extracts from the papers,
the compiler transferred much of Irving's personality to his
pages. Although Pierre Irving told tales of the larks in his
uncle's young manhood, the portrait confirmed the features
of the genial gentleman and romantic story-teller which
readers had derived from Irving's essays and short stories.
The life was less formal and admiring than many family
biographies, but later research has shown that it was omissive and incomplete. The great value of the four volumes
lay in the source material they contained.

Despite the distrust which clings to family biographies, no
one has a better right to compile a biography of a man than
his wife or child. This prerogative counts for little if it is
not supplemented with technical proficiency and fulfillment
of the twofold obligation which a family biographer owes to
his kin and to readers. These requisites appear in *Nathaniel
Hawthorne and His Wife* (2 vols., 1884), which was written by the son Julian. The work is a narrative of the father's
life and an intimate picture of the Hawthorne household.
"This biography will not be found to err on the side of
reticence," Julian Hawthorne said in the preface. He added
that the selection of the material to be used had been governed by taste rather than by discretion. The biography was
not published until twenty years after Hawthorne's death,
a circumstance which probably affected the nature of the
work. The biographer did not attempt to explain the novel-

ist's genius or to make a critical study of his writings. Although Julian Hawthorne had a mass of family papers and his own knowledge to draw upon, he was forced to use the recollections of others in the earlier part of his book. This led him unwittingly to exaggerate the conditions of Hawthorne's "strange childhood" and his solitude. The biographer did not, at least, try to mold the novelist into a stereotyped pattern or to make him a completely exceptional individual. Valuable as the biography has been as a sourcebook, the character and life of Hawthorne have needed the benefit of more extensive research and more objective biographers.

Before Julian Hawthorne's book was published, George P. Lathrop wrote an interpretation of the romancer and his work which ranks high among the critical studies of Hawthorne. Lathrop was Hawthorne's son-in-law, but so far as his point of view and treatment of his subject were concerned, he might have been a complete stranger to the family. "I do not enter upon this attempt as a mere literary performance," Lathrop said, "but have been assisted in it by an inward impulse, a consciousness of sympathy with the subject, which I may consider a sort of inspiration." Lathrop's sympathy was amply supported by a knowledge of Hawthorne's writings and an understanding of their meaning and implication. *A Study of Hawthorne* (1876) was a personal interpretation which can not meet with unanimous agreement, but it explains its figure with skill, wisdom and justice.

The men of letters of the early nineteenth century did not write formal autobiographies. They left voluminous material about their inner and outer lives—Emerson and Thoreau in their *Journals,* Thoreau in *Walden,* and Hawthorne in his

Note-Books, to cite three instances—but they composed no self-narratives in the Franklin tradition.[2]

The biography of Longfellow (2 vols., 1886) which was compiled by his brother Samuel is arranged in the loose form of an autobiography. It is a chronological mosaic of extracts, passages and whole units carefully chosen from the poet's diaries, correspondence and other papers, and held together by a slender narrative supplied by the biographer. This resembles the bare skeleton of James Boswell's method, but Samuel Longfellow's work lacks the unity, vitality and interpretation of the *Life of Johnson.* It is but a partial autobiography and presents only the external side of the poet's life. Although Longfellow revealed much of his inner nature in his lyrical poems, he did not record that side in his diaries. He gave a clue to the absence of such entries when he wrote: "If one were only sure that one's journal would never be seen by any one, and never get into print, how different the case would be! But death picks the locks of all portfolios and throws the contents into the street for the public to scramble after."

Unlike most of his contemporaries, Emerson was the subject of an extended biography (1881) while he was living. This book by George W. Cooke was intended to be an interpretation of Emerson's philosophy, but the author used much narrative and portrait material in his study. Cooke wrote "as a disciple rather than as a critic, not because he sees nothing to criticise, but because he feels that in this way alone can full justice be done the subject." (From the Preface) The official—and long the standard—biography, *A Memoir of Ralph Waldo Emerson* (1887) was compiled in two volumes by James E. Cabot, the literary executor,

---

[2]William Cullen Bryant wrote a fragmentary autobiography, which was used by his biographer Parke Godwin.

five years after Emerson had died. This life was a factual narrative written without additional interpretation or criticism. As Cabot had access to Emerson's journals, letters and other papers which had not been published previously, his biography became both a valuable source-book and a reliable guide to the external side of Emerson's career.

II

Occupations and fields of achievement have served as unifying links for many series of biographies. Authors, statesmen, actors, military leaders, pioneers and patriots, and notable individuals in other categories have been brought together on common bases. The lives in a series are usually written at the request of its editor-in-chief or a publisher. In some cases a prospective contributor is allowed to choose the figure he will depict. Each biography is generally limited in extent to one volume. The series scheme has occasionally been condemned as "commercialized biography," but there is nothing wrong in such an enterprise *per se*. Biographies with the glow of artistry, as well as "industrious compilations," have been written to order. The chief drawback, when it exists, consists in laying upon the contributors certain conditions such as manner of treatment and length which prevent full freedom of individualized workmanship. A biographical series to be successful demands at the outset the union of the right author with the right subject. The single volumes have the same requisites of their art as if they were to be written independently. No series yet published has had the same degree of achievement throughout all its volumes. Variation in skill of execution has been inevitable. When they are well done, the units in a series are useful as introductions to their subjects, and they serve respective readers in other ways.

The American Men of Letters Series, which was a counterpart of the English Men of Letters, was established in
1881 under the general editorship of Charles Dudley Warner. The series, which began with a life of Washington
Irving by Warner, was continued into the early 1900s and
finally comprised some twenty-five volumes. With the exception of Franklin, the subjects were authors of the nineteenth century. The selection of individual biographers was
wisely made. The series became a collection of much value
for the biographical information it contained and in many
cases for the critical judgment of the contributors. Among
the lives in the series which stand out at the present time
are those of Poe and Hawthorne by George E. Woodberry,
of Walt Whitman by Bliss Perry, and of James Russell Lowell by Ferris Greenslet. Thomas R. Lounsbury contributed
the first biography to be published of James Fenimore
Cooper (1883), who had died thirty years before. A leading
reason for this delay in the publication of a life of the novelist was Cooper's injunction to his family not to authorize any
biography of him. Lounsbury did not have access to the
family papers, but he gathered sufficient material for an account of Cooper's career. He devoted a large part of the
biography to criticism of Cooper's works.

The American Statesmen Series, which was inaugurated
in 1882 under the general editorship of John T. Morse, Jr.,
eventually comprised the biographies of twenty-eight men
whose careers lay in the eighteenth and first half of the nineteenth century. Morse was an exceptionally gifted biographer. He contributed to the series lives of Franklin, John
Adams, John Quincy Adams, Jefferson and Lincoln. The
work on Lincoln (2 vols., 1893) was the most discriminating
study of its figure that had been made. Morse was not affected by certain factors which had influenced earlier biog-

raphers of Lincoln. He did not feel the uncritical idolatry of the eulogists or the indignation of Herndon or the political loyalty of Nicolay and Hay. Morse carried out his biography in a more detached manner, and his work did not suffer from the veneration he had for his hero. Although he did not fully explain the nature of Lincoln's character, his interpretation was more revealing and trustworthy than preceding portraits. Morse's life was written with a critical analysis of data which had not previously appeared in Lincoln biography.

The life of Washington in the American Statesmen Series (2 vols., 1889) was done in a new style. The author, Henry Cabot Lodge, avoided the traditional treatment which his subject had received for ninety years and replaced the idealized figure of a demigod with a realistic portrait of a human being. The biography was corrective rather than critical. Lodge tried to destroy the Weemsian myths and other erroneous views of Washington. As a wholehearted partisan of Washington and the Federalist doctrine, Lodge believed that the unembellished truth—as he saw the truth—would do ample justice to his hero. The book contained a vivid picture of the time and a clear-cut analysis of the affairs with which Washington was connected. This matter was necessarily presented in a condensed form. The publication of the biography coincided with the centennial observance of Washington's inauguration.

Other lives of special distinction in this series were those of Thomas Hart Benton (1886) by Theodore Roosevelt, of Andrew Jackson (1882) by William G. Sumner, and of John Marshall (1885) by Allan B. Magruder. The life of John Randolph (1882) by Henry Adams was marked by the author's antipathy to his figure. Adams made it clear that he shared the dislike which his ancestors John and John

Quincy had felt toward Randolph. He also admitted that the fiery Virginian had had reason to hate the Adamses. The biographer granted that Randolph had certain qualities of merit, but the general tone of the book was inimical and censorious.

Of higher standing and far more value than the *Randolph* among Adams' works is the life of Albert Gallatin (1879). Gallatin was secretary of the treasury in Jefferson's cabinet and was surpassed only by Alexander Hamilton as an executive of finance. This life, which is not in a series, has long been recognized as a great political biography, and it has earned the status of being definitive. Henry Adams felt a strong admiration for his figure. Gallatin "was the most fully and perfectly equipped statesman we can show," the biographer declared on one occasion. He did not allow this esteem to alter his transcript of the Gallatin record. The admiration was governed by a characteristic restraint and was fortified by the best technical principles. Adams depicted his hero in vast detail on a broad canvas. The biography runs to almost seven hundred pages. He employed the method of making Gallatin his own biographer to a large extent, quoting copiously from the man's letters and papers, and bringing his personality and acts clearly before the reader. The author skillfully supplied the necessary parts of the narrative and the background material. The work is a notably felicitous union of biographer and subject.

Chapter XI

DISSENT AND CONVENTION IN THE 1890s

At the beginning of that decade which has been variously labeled gay, yellow and mauve, biography had been written in this country for two hundred and thirty-two years. During those centuries American life-literature had been devoid of the eventful episodes which occur from time to time in the field of letters. From its inception in the Colonial era biography had been in a state of flux, but the evolution of the art had proceeded with a quiet and orderly transition from one stage to the next.

In the Colonial and Revolutionary periods theological disputes and political quarrels had brought on torrents of words, but no pamphlet wars had raged among the biographers. In the nineteenth century Emerson had summoned the American scholar to new duties, and Whitman had proclaimed a new order in poetry; but no rebels like the Concord Sage and the Good Gray Poet sounded biographic declarations of independence.[1] No innovator like Howells in

---

[1] Whitman had expressed dissatisfaction with biographical portraiture, but writing lives was not a part of his literary purpose. See Horace Traubel, *With Walt Whitman in Camden*, Vol. I, pp. 108, 398.

realism had paved the way for audacious young men of the
next generation. James Parton had avoided the spell of the
halo and had stressed the human attributes of his characters, but he established no new school of writers. Before the
twentieth century no indecorous youngsters or cynical intel-
lectuals had risen to upset the conventional concepts of the
national heroes. American biography before 1900 had never
felt the agitation of revolutionary forces. As the nineteenth
century drew to an end, the calm began to be ruffled.

The decade of the 1890s was a period of striking transition in American life, a finale as well as a prelude, a time
of protest and revolt, of prophecy and progress. It was a
decade of unrest and discontent, of experimentation, of fresh
theories and new philosophies which were to mature and
bear fruit in the first thirty years of the new century. The
ferment which was stirring the existing order in politics,
economics, social thinking and letters appeared in milder
form in the realm of life-literature. The insurgents in those
fields — men like Benjamin O. Flower, Henry D. Lloyd,
Jacob Riis and Stephen Crane—had counterparts, fewer in
number, less vehement but earnestly active, among the
biographers.

Symptomatic of the time was the voice of dissent that was
raised by Paul Leicester Ford, historian and bibliographer,
and a specialist in the era of the American Revolution. Like
other judicial investigators who had scrutinized the Washington papers, Ford was aware of the discrepancy between
the actual man and the sanctified figure of the earlier biographers. Unlike his predecessors, he was unwilling to ignore
or sanction the common idea of Washington. He marveled
that keen, practical Americans should engage in the ancient
form of hero-building. He believed that the process by
which historical personages were canonized had done more

harm than good. The myth-makers had transformed great human leaders into isolated statues. Washington in particular had suffered by this treatment. Impelled by the desire to restore the real man, Ford made an intimate study of his subject which he called *The True George Washington* (1896).

The volume is made up of twelve essays which bear such titles as Physique, Education, Farmer and Proprietor, Citizen and Office-Holder. So far as possible the author used the Boswellian method of letting his subject speak for himself, "in the hope that his own words would convey a greater sense of [his] personality." Ford also quoted extensively from other manuscripts of Washington's period. The biography embodied a conception of Washington as he appeared to his associates and the people of his time. Ford laid his emphasis on character and individuality. He did not seek to evaluate the military leader or the statesman in the light of historical perspective. He said little directly about the historical significance of his figure. Neither did the author make Washington a victim of his dislike of the old style of hero-worship. He simply presented the findings of his research in an impartial manner, with no attempt to make up the reader's mind in advance. The book is open to objection if one insists that a biography must have the chronological structure. The essay form which Ford used did not allow him to show Washington's life in sequence or to achieve the design of a finished portrait. The reader, nevertheless, obtains a realistic picture of Washington.

Ford was a deliberate humanizer. He anticipated the later followers of Lytton Strachey only in his purpose and not in their method or style. He was reconstructional in his manner rather than interpretative. He evolved no new technique which might have excited the enthusiasm of readers and brought forth a school of imitators. He did, however, prove that a corrective biography could be written without radical measures. The book was well received by the public and has been widely read.

Ford also compiled another biography, *The Many-Sided Franklin* (1899), by the same plan he had used in the *Washington*. The work may be praised for the same merits and is open to the same demurrer, on account of its essay form, as the preceding book.

Other evidence of "the check which is being given to our peculiar myth-making" appeared in the preface of *The True Benjamin Franklin* (1899) by Sydney George Fisher, a lawyer of Philadelphia and a writer on American historical subjects. Fisher described a condition and spoke a prophecy. He said in part: "This assumption that our people are children who must not be told the eternal truths of human nature, but deceived into goodness by wooden heroes and lay figures, seems, fortunately, to be passing away, and in a few years it will be a strange phase to look back upon."

Unlike Ford's life of Washington, the biography by Fisher was a subjective portrayal. The author set out in an aggressively corrective mood to re-appraise Franklin. It was the traditional method of hero-worship and not the man that Fisher disliked. His aversion to the old style led him to shift the emphasis and stress Franklin's "errata" and shortcomings. The book met a mixed reception from reviewers and readers. The *Saturday Review* (of London) praised the biographer for making known the true Franklin. The New York *Nation* lamented the many errors in the book. The Chicago *Dial* classed the work as an example of lampblack biography.

The opinions held by Ford and Fisher were not the views of these authors alone. The *Nation* said that Ford had expressed what was undoubtedly a general feeling in the country at the time. His lives of Washington and Franklin were not biographies of the highest order. Yet they were, with Fisher's *Franklin*, significant signs of the period. They represented the early phase of a new chapter in American biography. The complaints made in the prefaces of these volumes were an indication of the growing reaction against the custom of making historical figures into saints. They were a symptom of the critical spirit with which the United States was to examine itself in the next century.

Another biography that manifested dissent was the life of Christopher Columbus (1891) by Justin Winsor, librarian of Harvard College and a leading historian. This work diverged sharply from the prevailing idea of its hero. The nature of the discoverer's career, with its setbacks and hardships and eventual success, had made him a favorite figure with American biographers. Owing largely to the lives written by Washington Irving and William H. Prescott, both of whom had extoled him, Columbus occupied a hallowed niche in the American pantheon. Winsor made a thorough examination of the available material and arrived at different conclusions from the previous authors. His interpretation of Columbus was iconoclastic, yet the portrait was balanced. Winsor pointed out deficiencies in the works of other authors and documented his study with evidence.

A corrective biography of the opposite kind was the life of Thomas Paine (2 vols., 1892) by Moncure D. Conway. This biography aimed to dispel detraction, not eulogy. The real character of Paine had been lost in a murk of abuse and falsehood even before his death in 1809. He had long been regarded in the public mind as a black sheep among the Revolutionary heroes. No genuine biography of the man had ever been written. In an effort to discover the true

Paine, Conway made a judicial investigation of the contemporary records and other sources of information. The biography was from its purpose largely a book of refutation, and the author became in a sense an advocate. The life bore the marks of honest presentation. It was a greatly needed contribution to American biography, although it did not settle the long controversy over its figure. The life opened a new chapter of lay and biographical interest in Paine.

The biographies of avowed dissent during the 90s, in numerical minority as they were, stood out from the conventional lives because they struck a new critical note and articulated opinions that were held by an increasing number of authors and readers. They reflected the process of change that was quickening its tempo at the end of the century. During the decade, however, other men were depicted from more temperate motives.

American biography received a product of high scholarship in the life of Napoleon Bonaparte by William M. Sloane, professor of history at Columbia University. The work, which was in four volumes (1896-97), made available to American readers the findings of recent research in the Napoleonic period. Sloane wrote from an objective viewpoint and observed an impartiality. The biography is of the life-and-times class, and the balance between the two parts is well maintained throughout. Sloane's portrayal of his hero is superior to his treatment of the background of the time. It has been unfortunate that this life of Napoleon is too long and too formal to have general reading. It is the kind of biography on which popularizers lean heavily.

A biography of George Washington (1896) by Woodrow Wilson, then professor of history at Princeton University, was a work of the life-and-background type. Wilson took special pains to picture the Virginia society from which the president came and to analyze the factors of heredity and environment which affected his character and career. The nature of these factors and the influence they exerted on the figure were clearly explained. The biography thus became a work of skillful interpretation from the particular viewpoint which the author adopted.

In *Cotton Mather: Puritan Priest* (1891) Barrett Wendell portrayed the divine as he appeared in his diaries and journals one hundred and fifty years after his death. The main difficulty in writing a rounded life of Cotton Mather is to unite in the right proportions and with the proper emphasis the contradictory qualities of the man. Wendell balanced the scales in reasonable fashion. The biography was tempered with a charitable tone, but Wendell did not adjust the lens of his scrutiny to magnify Mather's virtues or minimize his faults.

A new chapter in Lincoln biography opened in the 90s. Samuel S. McClure, seeking a broad subject of general interest for the new magazine that bore his name, commissioned Ida M. Tarbell to make fresh research in the Lincoln country and write a series of articles for the magazine. The project became to Miss Tarbell far more than a mere assignment. For years afterward she remained an ardent student of Lincoln. "She was the pioneer scientific investigator whose work foretold the revelation of Lincoln as he really was."[2] She discovered new material of importance, and she added a new phase to the study of Lincoln by stressing the influence of the frontier on the man. Miss Tarbell published a life of Lincoln in 1900 and other books in later years.

---

[2]Thomas, *Portrait for Posterity*, p. 201.

CHAPTER XII

THE ADVANCE OF "PURE" BIOGRAPHY
(1900-1920)

The mutations in biographical practice which had begun
in the latter part of the nineteenth century became more
widespread and pronounced as the new century advanced.
Standards which rested on the recognized usage of a hundred years in this country continued to give way before the
play of new forces. Chief among these were the spirit of
free inquiry and the vitalizing power of realism. Moreover,
the feeling of social democracy was creating interest in common men and their affairs, and was emphasizing the worth
of the individual. The popularization of learning was
spreading a desire for knowledge that was presented in a
simple and palatable form.

These four factors caused numerous changes in the writing of biography. The old principle that only good should
be said of the dead, lost favor. The solemn eulogistic note
was rarely heard. More and more did reality replace myth.
Greater emphasis was placed on interpretation and the rev-

elation of character. More conscious use was made of psychological principles. The manner in which men were portrayed moved toward the familiar. Biography became less formal and more worldly. It acquired a larger degree of verisimilitude. American life-literature had never been the exclusive estate of great men; in the twentieth century the range of figures was extended still further, and no type of character, it seemed, was denied recognition. Life-writing had likewise been a free occupation of mixed ranks and skills; it now became more crowded and diverse in its workers. The general interest in the subject increased, and readers multiplied in all classes of society. American biography thus entered a new stage in its development.

II

The leading lives that were written in the first twenty years of the century gave evidence that another order in biographical writing had arrived. Today there is an aura of permanence around some of these books. They have stood the test of critical scrutiny for thirty years and more — a significant criterion in the field of biography. A number of major works that were published between 1900 and 1920 are considered here.

The appointment of Albert Bigelow Paine as official biographer to Mark Twain was said in 1912 to be "the greatest Boswellian instance in modern times." There was much truth to this superlative assertion. Clemens was an exceptionally felicitous subject. There was, to be sure, no romantic mystery about the man, no baffling enigma, no raging controversy. But he was an intensely human figure, volatile in temperament and uninhibited in thought and action. His personality was engaging, and his nature complex. His life had been filled with lively adventure of all sorts. He was important for his achievement in the field of letters. His career was woven into a unique period of American history. The subject and the biographer worked together on the project for several years before Clemens died in 1910. Paine completed the undertaking alone, and the biography of three volumes and sixteen hundred pages was published in 1912. In this standard life there was excellent balance be-tween the autobiographic contribution of the figure and the sympathetic objectivity of the biographer. The narrative showed how "the man of the frontier became, without losing his essence and tang, quite literally the man of the world."

When Benjamin Franklin wrote his autobiography, lack of time and failing health forced him to leave unrecorded the last thirty years of his life. Even the middle years of his career deserved more detail than he gave them. As a result of this missing matter, many biographers since Jared Sparks have undertaken to tell the story of the man's whole life and to amplify the portions he did narrate. The portrayal of Franklin on a large scale has been done best by James Parton and by authors of the twentieth century. The challenge which Franklin makes to modern biographers is not to solve a mystery or to fathom motives of conduct or to appraise unrecognized achievements. The invitation is rather the opportunity to re-create a diverse individuality that is essentially timeless and a supreme career that has no counterpart. This was done by William Cabell Bruce in *Benjamin Franklin, Self-Revealed* (2 vols., 1917) with sound scholarship, keen understanding and skilled craftsmanship.

Men whose careers are bound up with contemporary happenings are seen to the best biographical advantage on broad canvases. They shape and are shaped by events. They take positions on great issues. They clash in controversies over principles of political policy. Mere references to these affairs in a biography are of small aid to the unversed layman. The events, issues and debates require explanation if the actors and the roles they played are to be fairly understood. These historical demands are well satisfied in *Life of John Marshall* (4 vols., 1916-19) by Albert J. Beveridge, without loss to the biographical portions of the work. Beveridge depicts Marshall as a lifelike human being who is not lost in the march of events through the pages. He interprets the Federalism of his figure and deals with the decisions of the chief justice which established precedents of far-reaching effects. He goes into the history of the cases which were carried to the Supreme Court and expounds the arguments they involved. Beveridge dramatized much of the biography and stressed the human interest that lay in his subject matter. A Federalist in his sympathies, he made Jefferson a foil to his central figure. Jefferson's place in the epoch is therefore better read in other biographies.

Biography of the old school sanctioned calculated partisanship in the lives of political personages. Echoes of the school are occasionally heard in later biographies, but partisanship in political lives today is more apt to be based on documentary evidence than emotional grounds. The art has been served more faithfully in the twentieth century. Two biographies in its early decades which show this advance are the lives of Andrew Jackson (2 vols., 1911) by John S. Bassett and of John C. Calhoun (2 vols., 1910) by William M. Meigs. These works are comprehensive in scope and impartial in the treatment of their figures. The portraits are rounded, and the narratives keep an even keel in the seas of political storms. Both biographies lack the vivid quality which was to appear in later lives of the two men.

Biographies that assemble the definite facts about a controversial figure and present them in veracious fashion are of great value for that reason alone. This is the status of *John Brown,* 1800-1859: *Biography Fifty Years After* (1910) by Oswald Garrison Villard. For years after his execution Brown was acclaimed as a saintlike martyr and denounced as a vainglorious fanatic. The contention had not subsided when Villard made an exhaustive study of the man and his career. Sympathetic as the biographer was toward his subject, he worked in the manner of a scientific investigator, gathering, sifting and weighing the evidence on both sides of the case. This material he compiled in a history of over seven hundred pages. In drawing his conclusions, Villard made no attack or defence of John Brown, and the biography hardly settled the controversy. The work is notable for its accuracy, honesty and fullness. The book would gain in readability if the author had combined more of the qualities of a literary artist with his proficiency as a scientific biographer.

The *Life and Times of Cavour* (2 vols., 1911) by William Roscoe Thayer presents the career and historical background of the statesman who molded the parts of Italy together and made that country a unified kingdom. Thayer was for years an ardent student of Italian history, and he was thoroughly conversant with the forces at work, the issues involved, and the men who were engaged in the struggle. He had the historian's skill in unfolding the complex panorama of events in a lucid manner, and the biographer's ability to make the characters real human beings. Thayer did not restrict his chronicle to political affairs alone. By necessity he treated the social, economic and religious forces which affected the course of Cavour's policies. A strong asset of the book is the order, arrangement and proportion which the author gave to the mass of material he selected for the drama he recorded. Thayer was strongly sympathetic to Cavour, and he often used his protagonist's point of view at the expense of Cavour's opponents and their side in the struggle. The work gained a kind of objectivity by being written by a biographer of a foreign country.

Two biographers of this period compiled lives of English authors. Wilbur L. Cross of Yale University wrote *History of Henry Fielding* (3 vols., 1918) and *Life and Times of Laurence Sterne* (2 vols., 1925). George M. Harper of Princeton wrote *William Wordsworth His Life, Works and Influence* (2 vols., 1916). (The *Sterne* was originally published in a much shorter version in one volume in 1909.) These biographies are comprehensive chronicles based on solid scholarship and produced from endless research and reading. In this way the biographers had lived for years with their subjects and knew them intimately. The three authors are pictured in the setting of their times. The books are filled with vignettes of their associates and other contemporaries, social and literary sidelights, anecdotes and chitchat. The style of the *Wordsworth* is more formal than that of the lives by Cross. All three biographies are definitive source-books and authoritative studies.

The *Life of Alice Freeman Palmer* (1908) by George Herbert Palmer is an appreciation written from affection to commemorate a radiant personality and to set forth an example of inspiration for others. The author did not allow these aims to alter the fidelity of his biography. Mrs. Palmer, a woman of great intellectual and spiritual endowments, was president of Wellesley College and a prominent worker in the field of women's education. The biography is more the portrait of a woman and a wife than the story of a career. The appreciation is written with a reserve that does not lessen its effect and with a frankness that makes the life an intimate revelation of character. Perhaps no other man has contributed to American biography "so charming and acceptable a book about his own wife." The author's skill as biographer and the sincerity of his purpose create a portrait that is human in the best sense of that term.

The publication of Emerson's *Journals* in ten volumes in the early part of the century made available a vast amount of new material. The journals, which Emerson kept for fifty-five years, were mainly the record of impressions, observations, reflections and opinions. Oscar W. Firkins made able use of the material in his study of Emerson (1915) which is both biographical and critical. The two portions of the book are divided about evenly. The whole work is subjective and presents an acute, thorough and fair interpretation of Emerson's career and writings. The interpretation is executed in a manner which harmonizes with the tone and substance of the philosopher's thought. The style of the biographer calls to mind the style of his subject. This similarity of expression is not often found in American biography.

Of all the biographies of European figures by American authors, the foremost is *The Life of Ludwig van Beethoven* by Alexander W. Thayer. The work was the product of an enthusiasm for the musician which Thayer formed in his student days at Harvard College in the early 1840s. The compilation of the biography became his life-task. He went to Europe to obtain his material firsthand and devoted forty years to research and writing. Thayer was consul at Trieste for thirty years, and in that post he had ample opportunity to travel about the continent, interviewing persons who had known Beethoven, searching records, and digging out data in libraries and other sources. At the time of his death in 1897 Thayer had written three volumes of the biography, but his great project was uncompleted. He wrote the life in

English, but it was first issued in Germany in translation, volume by volume, and was soon recognized as a classic. Thayer never saw the biography in published form in his own language.

The appearance of the first German volume in 1866 had excited strong interest in the study of Beethoven. Other students joined Thayer in the field, and a vast amount of new material was discovered. Over eighty men subsequently contributed to the final German edition, which was published in five volumes from 1908 to 1911.

The first American edition of the biography, which was published in three volumes in 1920-21, was a composite work made from Thayer's original manuscript, the fruits of the labors of the German editors and collaborators, and a mass of data which Thayer had collected. All this matter was revised and edited and completed with painstaking care over a period of ten summers by Henry Edward Krehbiel, a music critic of New York who had known Thayer. The expenses of publication were borne by the Beethoven Association of New York. "A group of American musicians devoted to this purpose the proceeds of a winter's season."[1]

In this first version in English, Mr. Krehbiel wrote, "is told for the first time in the language of the great biographer the true story of the man Beethoven—his history stripped of the silly sentimental romance with which early writers and their later imitators and copyists invested it so thickly that the real humanity, the humanliness of the composer, has never been presented to the world. In this biography there appears the veritable Beethoven set down in his true environment of men and things—the man as he actually was, the man as he himself, like Cromwell, asked to be shown for the information of posterity." Thayer's biography is of

[1]Van Wyck Brooks, *New England: Indian Summer*, p. 167

the narrative-portrait type and does not have a critical analysis of Beethoven's work.[2]

---

[2]For accounts of Thayer's life of Beethoven see the article by Mr. Krehbiel in the *Musical Quarterly*, Vol. 3, pp. 629-640, October 1917; Brooks, *New England: Indian Summer*, pp. 165-168; and the sketch of Thayer by John Tasker Howard in the *Dictionary of American Biography*. Krehbiel's article was written while the manuscript of the biography was locked in the vaults of a publishing house during World War I, awaiting a better time for publication.

CHAPTER XIII

THE PSYCHOLOGIC METHOD: GAMALIEL BRADFORD

The manner in which biographers study and interpret "the invisible life" of their characters is commonly referred to as the psychologic method. This procedure was not an innovation in the twentieth century. The rudiments of analysis are as old as biography itself. Whenever biographers of any age have tried to explain the mental processes and inner motivations of their subjects, they have been psychologic in manner. Often in the past they did not seem to be conscious of any scientific procedure. Often too their consideration of the springs of action was only a minor part of their purpose. Whether undeliberate or incidental, however, the procedure bore the marks of psychologic inquiry. As such it appeared in the memoirs of the Colonial time and in many of the lives of the nineteenth century. As biographical exposition later felt the growing interest in the new principles of scientific investigation, it developed a more intricate and subtle form of interpretation. The attempt to explain the why and wherefore of human behavior became a recognized part of biographical practice. The newness of the procedure in the twentieth century lies in the biographer's studied use of the method and in the emergence of the type of "psychologic biography" in which analysis of "the inner man" is a leading feature of the author's purpose. Biographers who use the method are cognizant of its possibilities and significance.

The psychologic method of interpretation has had one great point of appeal. It seemed to be a medium that would furnish the missing ultimate in biographical study. Writers and readers who had a passion to learn what had hitherto been hidden or unknown about famous men and women felt that psychology was the key with which to fathom the enigma of personality and solve unanswered questions relating to the characters and careers of the figures. Although some biographers granted that the method was qualified by a lack of certainty in the discoveries, there was a strong belief that the findings were approximate if not absolute. This faith in the benefits of pyschology was reinforced in some circles of biography by the principles of psychoanalysis. The Freudian system seemingly enabled a life-writer to ascertain the "deeper motives and feelings and purposes which the individual conceals not only from others but even from himself."

The hazards involved in applying the psychologic method are great. Unlike the novelist and the dramatist, the biographer, as has been said, must confine his study to an indi‘vidual who has actually lived. A biographical subject can not always be questioned, and if that were possible, he might have an imperfect knowledge of his consciousness and conduct. Then again, does the biographer possess all the necessary data in the case at hand? Are letters or pages of private journals missing, or the needed testimony of witnesses lacking? Are there relevant circumstances of which the biographer is totally unaware? Even if the data are complete and trustworthy, what deductions may be correctly drawn from them? Volumes of subjective biography are filled with conflicting points of interpretation. Although an author may not prove that he is right, it is sometimes difficult to refute his conclusions. In some instances this may be done by making documented rebuttal or by showing that his reasoning is false. Furthermore, a biographer should not be misled by his unverified preferences or by a pet theory which can not be established. In short, psychologic diagnosis should be made judiciously from hard scrutiny of the entire data. The distance from the raw facts to the final conclusions is interpretatively great. To go the way successfully demands the intricate qualities which make up the biographic sixth sense. For all that, the biographer may still feel with Gamaliel Bradford "the terrible uncertainty" of the ground beneath his feet.

The interest in the latent processes of human nature is not limited to biographies which are labeled psychologic. The desire to know the why and wherefore of external actions is strong today among writers and readers. The principle of analysis and revelation is in widespread use among subjective biographers, although many of them employ it only as a lesser part of their purpose without any scientific intent. In its application to biographical study the psychologic method has worked for both good and ill. It has been a means of making plausible if not definitive contributions to our knowledge of men and women. Conversely, it has done incalculable harm by circulating flimsy conjectures, false theories and unfounded conclusions. The method is a two-edged tool whose efficacy is governed by the value of the available evidence and the interpretative skill of the biographer.

II

In one of his critical articles on the art of biography, Gamaliel Bradford speaks of "the thoughtful biographer who gives his life to probing more and more deeply into the fundamental reality of human nature, not for scandal, not for notoriety, but with the sole object of extending a little further the substantial domain of truth."[1] In that sentence, consciously or not, Bradford stated his own aim and epitomized his own procedure. During the last twenty years of his life, from 1912 to 1932, he assiduously sought the biographical truth which lay in "the marks and indications of the souls of men." He analyzed human conduct, exploring the springs of action, and he dissected the "vast complex" of individuality for its characteristic qualities and significant manifestations. His findings he converted into psychological portraits—studies which on the whole were markedly successful attempts to depict character and to reveal the "subtle mystery and secret of personality."

Bradford was the first American biographer to make deliberate and specialized use of the psychological method. A follower of Sainte-Beuve, whom he hailed as his master and model, Bradford has been the leading writer and exponent of psychography in this country. He adopted that term to describe his own genre before he knew that George Saintsbury had already used the word in discussing the work of Sainte-Beuve. Bradford preferred to call his studies "psychographs" rather than portraits. Believing that it was misleading to carry the terms of one art into another, Bradford argued that a portrait painter could represent a man at only one moment in his career. The psychographer, on the

---

[1]"Sainte-Beuve and Biography," *Saturday Review of Literature,* Vol. VII, p. 953, July 11, 1931.

other hand, endeavors to give his reader the sum total of as many particular moments as he can. Bradford defined psychography as "the condensed, essential, artistic presentation of character." In preparation for the picture, the psychographer, after infinite reading and long study, selects the attitudes, actions, utterances and other manifestations of character which are significant, distinguishing and habitual of the entire life and individuality of his subject. Especially does he watch for the intimate touches and illuminating sidelights which reveal the mind and the heart. This material he weaves interpretatively, without regard for chronological sequence, into a whole which will be a typical composite of the figure's character.

Bradford wanted to analyze his figures in a methodical manner and to separate and extract from the "weltering chaos" of individuality the qualities he needed for his portraits. He accordingly studied his subjects in their relation to such universal forces as love, ambition, money and religion. What was the particular effect of each of these elements, and how was the effect manifested? At the same time Bradford heeded any other personal marks and traits which would contribute to his purpose. By drawing his portraits from such data, he made his men and women well-defined members of the human family, and he also individualized them by showing the interplay of their personal qualities and the common denominators of human experience.

Bradford used his method with painstaking care, restraint and subtlety. He searched dispassionately for the truth, and out of his analysis and reflection he wrought soul-portraits which exhibited with vivid strokes the complex elements of human nature. In the gallery of some one hundred and fourteen psychographs which Bradford composed there is inevitably a variation in quality and a difference in the extent of agreement which readers feel with the features of the individual portraits and with the conclusions of the biographer.

The psychograph is a highly subjective form. From the moment he begins to choose the distinguishing qualities of his subject until he completes his interpretation, the equation of the author is actively at work. It is in the mirror of Bradford's temperament, which is everywhere in evidence, that the reader views the sitter. Bradford exercised freely the functions of judge and critic. He could be gentle or spirited or ironical. If he granted prejudices at times, he was generally sympathetic and patient toward his figures. He was shrewd and discerning in his perceptions, broad and humane in his interests, considered and honest in his judgments. One senses his effort to do justice to his subjects to the full extent of his method. Bradford added to his technical process a style that had simplicity, clarity and polish.

Bold as he was in his purpose and persistent in his undertaking, Bradford felt humility in his work. Time and again in his portraits and in his criticism of biography, he referred to the difficulty of truly understanding character and of recreating a human personality. He recognized the elusiveness of the qualities he sought, the difficulty in pronouncing judgment, the impossibility of saying the final word. Haunted by the uncertainty of interpretation and reluctant to risk untrue assertions, Bradford blurred the lines of his portraits at times. If he had ignored the frailties of human judgment and assumed a certain sureness, his portraits would have been drawn more positively. Whether they would have been more accurate is open to question.

Bradford, in his own words, "literally stumbled into the line of biographical work" after a long period of failure and discouragement in writing poems, novels and plays. During that time he had been beset by chronic ill-health, but the

ambition to be an author had driven him on. Just as
it seemed that he should abandon literary labor altogether,
he published a volume entitled *Lee the American* (1912), in
which he applied the technique of psychography he had
learned from Sainte-Beuve. Bradford was then forty-nine
years old. The critical recognition and success of the book
led him to continue his work in analytical portraiture. In
the subsequent years of his life he filled a vast gallery with
canvases, mainly of American men and women. All this was
accomplished while he remained an invalid and was nar-
rowly restricted in his reading and writing.

Bradford depicted men of the Civil War period in twin
volumes—*Confederate Portraits* (1914): Joseph E. Johnston, J. E. B. Stuart, Alexander H. Stephens and others;
and *Union Portraits* (1916): George B. McClellan, William
T. Sherman, Edwin M. Stanton and others. He made sev-
eral series of panels of women: *Portraits of Women* (1916),
Portraits of American Women (1919), *Wives* (1925), and
Daughters of Eve (1930). Among the figures in these volumes are Lady Mary Montagu, Jane Austen, Mrs. Pepys,
Abigail Adams, Harriet Beecher Stowe, Emily Dickinson,
Mrs. Abraham Lincoln, Mrs. Benedict Arnold, Theodosia
Burr, Catherine the Great, George Sand, Sarah Bernhardt.
A Naturalist of Souls (1917) contains studies of the poetry
of John Donne, Anthony Trollope, Alexander Dumas and
other essays.

In *American Portraits* (1922) Bradford added to his gal-
lery Mark Twain, Henry Adams, Sidney Lanier, James
McNeill Whistler, James G. Blaine, Grover Cleveland,
Henry James and Joseph Jefferson. In *Damaged Souls*
(1923) he anatomized Benedict Arnold, Thomas Paine,
Aaron Burr, John Randolph of Roanoke, John Brown, P. T.
Barnum and Benjamin F. Butler. Among the characters in

Bare Souls (1924) were Voltaire, Charles Lamb, John Keats and Gustave Flaubert. Bradford assembled portraits of some nineteenth-century Americans — Webster, Clay, Calhoun, Horace Greeley, Edwin Booth — in *As God Made Them* (1929), and he turned his attention to a varied group of later figures — Theodore Roosevelt, Woodrow Wilson, Thomas A. Edison, Henry Ford, Nikolai Lenin, Benito Mussolini and Calvin Coolidge—in *The Quick and the Dead* (1931). For the collection entitled *Saints and Sinners* (1932) he chose Caesar Borgia, Saint Francis of Assisi, Casanova, Thomas à Kempis, Talleyrand, Fénelon and Byron.

Bradford wrote three long lives: *The Soul of Samuel Pepys* (1924), *Darwin* (1926), and *Dwight L. Moody: A Worker in Souls* (1927).

After the death of Bradford there were published *Biography and the Human Heart* (1932), which contained portraits of Longfellow, Walt Whitman, Jones Very and others, and *Elizabethan Women* (1936), which was mainly a study of women characters in Elizabethan literature.[2]

Bradford was an enthusiastic advocate and a clear interpreter of the art of biography. No other American biographer has written at greater length on the subject. Bradford set forth his conception of its philosophical and technical principles in various essays which collectively form an exegesis of the art in general and a statement of his own creed and methods.[3]

He stressed the didactic and inspirational value of bio-

[2]See *Biography and the Human Heart* for a list of psychographs by Bradford.

[3]See especially "Psychography" in *A Naturalist of Souls* (1917); "The Art of Biography" in *Saturday Review of Literature*, Vol. I, pp. 769-770, May 23, 1925, and "Sainte-Beuve and Biography" in *Saturday Review of Literature*, Vol. VII, pp. 953-954, July 11, 1931.

graphy. The real basis of the subject, he maintained, is the universal desire to know the lives and souls of other human beings. We seek this knowledge because it illuminates our own lives and helps us to live them. "The study of others, as bearing upon ourselves," Bradford wrote, "that is the real secret." Although this was his thesis, he was not an avowed teacher or moralist. He was content to let the character he re-created communicate its own light and influence. He was an artist for the sake of his art—a naturalist of souls for the sake of psychography.

Although Bradford reiterated the enigma of personality, he left little if anything in the way of puzzle about himself. Through his portraits and biographical criticism, his daily journal which ran to some 1,400,000 words, and his letters to some five thousand correspondents, Bradford piled up huge material for a precise psychograph. His adventures, however, were of the mind and spirit rather than the body. Like Thoreau, who said he had traveled far in his native village of Concord, Bradford traveled far in his study in Wellesley Hills. There for twenty years he found his way in and out of the labyrinth of souls by the multiple threads of industry, humaneness, conscience and artistic integrity. If he did not solve all the enigmas which lay along his path, he traveled the maze wisely and well.

Chapter XIV

THE REVOLT IN THE 1920s

By 1920 the principle of critical realism was firmly established in biographical practice. The recent works of high
calibre had shown a clear-sighted awareness of objectives
and craftsmanship that met the demands of the new method
and the new consciousness. These marks of improvement
were reflected in smaller degree among biographies of lesser
rank. During the first two decades of the century the departure from the eulogistic and omissive style of portraiture
had continued steadily without fanfare or conflict. Near 1920
there was fresh dissent—stronger and more widespread than
that of the 90s—which quickly developed into a strong and
lively movement. A throng of new biographers appeared,
impatient with the existing order, flushed with fresh aims
and methods, and bent on writing lives in their own way.

The new movement ran its meteoric course beside the
established current of life-writing. While the insurgents
were in eruption, the authors who were already engaged in
corrective portraiture continued their work in a more orderly and less spectacular fashion. The dissenters drew an

incentive from the examples of foreign biographers. The other authors belonged rather to the current which had its inception in the various forces of the late nineteenth century. They bore a stronger relationship to the line of tradition, but the tradition which had cast off the extraneous aims of biography and become invigorated by the critical realism. The two currents were not wholly separate and distinct, nor were the writers in the two categories unlike in all respects. As workers in the perennial practice of re-interpretation, they recognized the need of reform. They differed in the source of the current in which they wrote and in the principles and methods which they employed.

The rise of the new movement made the 1920s the most turbulent and the most controversial period in American biography. The state of affairs which prevailed during those years was without precedent in the field.

For the time being the insurgents drew the spotlight of popular interest. Whoso would be a biographer must be a non-conformist, was the tacit slogan behind their work. Conspicuous in the upheaval were the iconoclasts, the ancestor-baiters, the "scientific analysts," and the fictional biographers. They rejected the conventional concepts of national heroes and made new evaluations by their own standards. They anatomized their victims with the alleged method of a psychologic clinic and fictionized their characters with the freedom of romantic novelists. The product of these writers gave rise to the term "the new biography." They were loudly applauded and roundly attacked. For a full decade the precincts of life-literature were filled with creative tumult and critical shouting. Biography was written and read in numbers that impressed even the American mind that is inured to startling statistics. In production and consumption those were the "boom days" in biography. The movement was an inevitable phenomenon in an age of turmoil.

The "new biography" had a fertile environment in which to grow. The soil was cultivated and prepared, and the atmosphere had a sharp skeptical tang. The time was ripe. In much of its mood the period was restless, cynical, disillusioned. Tradition was suspect if not rejected; former codes were unsettled; experiment was welcome. Authors with minds kindred to the dissenters—Sinclair Lewis, Carl Sandburg, H. L. Mencken, to name but three—were at work in the adjacent fields of fiction, poetry and criticism. The time-honored principles of biography had been challenged. The reticences and omissions of the old style were being corrected. When the 1920 decade opened, biography was in a flexible condition and was easily susceptible to the attacks of the insurgents. Their equipment was reinforced with fresh and tempting tools for the study of their subjects. The sciences of physics and biology offered them new avenues of approach to the interpretation of the individual. Psychology gave them the Freudian system of psychoanalysis with which to probe their characters. And they found, first in the work of Lytton Strachey and closely after in that of André Maurois and Emil Ludwig, alluring and imitable models which might conceivably have been sent to them by the patron saint of biographers.

II

Strachey kindled the movement with his two books, *Eminent Victorians* (New York, 1918) and *Queen Victoria* (New York, 1921). The former volume contained long essays on Henry Edward, Cardinal Manning, Florence Nightingale, Dr. Thomas Arnold and General Charles George Gordon. In the short preface of *Eminent Victorians* Strachey stated his creed and made an indictment of Victorian biography. He deprecated the customary "two fat volumes" of that period, "with their ill-digested masses of material, their slipshod style, their tone of tedious panegyric, their lamentable lack of selection, of detachment, of design."

The features of Strachey's biographies were the exact opposite of these defects. "A becoming brevity," he wrote, "which excludes everything that is redundant and nothing that is significant . . . is the first duty of the biographer." His biographies were composed on the principle of a strict economy. They are marked by a vigorous selection of matter that is pithy, expressive, often picturesque, at times diabolically significant. The details, incidents and little revelations of character are knitted into balanced parts. These are arranged in a symmetrical design whose pattern suggests the structure of a well-built novel or drama. The earlier "tone of tedious panegyric" became in a biography by Strachey a mood of radiant disenchantment. Strachey's style, which was his main distinction, was a source of delight to his readers and "a despair to his imitators." It is clear, fluent, unlabored, brilliant, quietly barbed. The style was an effective instrument for the expression of his biographical creed even if it was not a congruous garb in which to portray characters like Cardinal Manning, Dr. Arnold and Queen Victoria.

The initiated and the ignorant both found delightful aesthetic experience in Strachey. But readability is not the sole virtue of a biography. The first test is its truth. The central characters in the essays of *Eminent Victorians* and the figure of the queen are lifelike enough to move in the most realistic novel; as subjects in biography they are partial portraits. They are the creatures of the author's calculated interpretation. He selected what he wanted to use. If the older biographers centered their attention on the virtues of their heroes, Strachey fixed his gaze on the vulnerabilities of his figures. A hero depicted by the older school could not lose in the court of portraiture; a subject in the hands of Strachey could not win. Time and again he made his characters condemn themselves out of their own mouths and acts. His "angelic irony" and satiric thrusts were deadly. The lives by Strachey are triumphs in the synthesis of his particular eclecticism. They lack the representative totality of valid biography. The truth in his biographies does not have the balance and proportion which the structure possesses. Strachey was an iconoclast, subtle but devastating; a psychologist whose exceptional insight did not miss the foibles of his characters; a quasi novelist who sprinkled his pages with plausible imaginings.

Strachey alone would have been a sufficient guide for the revisionists. His *Eminent Victorians* and *Queen Victoria* contained all the elements which his followers needed. But the writers in the new mode were blessed with other examples from Europe. In *Ariel* (New York, 1923), a study of the poet Shelley by Maurois, they saw vividly demonstrated the use of the author's imagination as a fictional expedient in biography. *Ariel* was a portrait drawn from a hypothesis that was seemingly developed less by factual data than by a rich imagination. The author said that he wrote the book as a means in some measure of deliverance for himself.[1]

The narrative read like a romantic novel. It was a short fictionized biography, facile and delectable, which did not tax the reader in any way. *Ariel* met with a popular success as great as that of Strachey's two books. To the writers of the 1920s it was a new genre whose potentiality was immediately recognized.

The work of Emil Ludwig, the German biographer, illus-

---

[1] See chapter "Biography as a Means of Expression" in *Aspects of Biography* (1929) by Maurois.

trated psychological analysis and dramatic treatment. Like
Plutarch, Ludwig made personality his quarry. He believed
that "the most trivial habit will often suggest the interpretation of some major trait of character." He interpreted
character "by the symptoms of its behavior." In explaining
his method, Ludwig said that he relied largely on his intuition. This faculty, it may be added to Ludwig's statement,
is a delicate and fallible tool, even when it is applied to
findings of long and painstaking research. When the intuition is employed as a special instrument of interpretation
without such investigation, the soundness of the method and
the authenticity of the resulting portrait are open to just
question. Ludwig's intuition did not operate with uniform
results on all the figures he portrayed. His work was very
uneven in quality. He studied some men more carefully than
others, and he had a larger capacity to understand certain
personalities.

Ludwig's biographies are dramas in prose. He made his
narratives dramatic in manner and substance. This form of
treatment is legitimate enough in itself. Deliberate concen-
tration on it, however, tends to curtail or eliminate non-
dramatic matter which is essential and to over-intensify the
inherently dramatic.

The effect of the psychological and dramatic method is to
give the reader vast enjoyment and an ostensible knowledge
of the inner workings of human nature. Ludwig's method
appears most fully and effectively in his lives of Napoleon,
Goethe and Bismarck. With them and other volumes he
met the popular success of Strachey and Maurois.[2]

---

[2]The first biography by Ludwig (the life of Napoleon) to be published in
the United States was not brought out until 1926. His influence on American
writers began later than that of Strachey and Maurois.

The consideration of Strachey, Maurois and Ludwig in the foregoing paragraphs has been confined to the main significance of their relationship to
American biography.

III

Strachey had the largest influence of contemporary authors on the new mode. His method seemed easy to imitate. His art concealed both the wide reading he had done in preparation and the intricate workmanship that lay behind his portraits. His motive was plain, and the mechanics of his formula were clear. The potentiality of his model was expanded by the examples of Maurois and Ludwig. It was obvious that this technique could be applied to American figures. A host of writers leaped at the opportunity. No American Strachey emerged from the movement. Without exception no writer who attempted to copy the Stracheyan method had the ability of the master or the gift of his artistry. Strachey has been unjustly blamed for the failures of his imitators. He should rather be censured for the limitations of his own shining but deluding model.

Various motives prompted the writers of the new school. The biographer's instinctive desire to re-interpret in his own way was stimulated by the challenge of the latest technique, which offered the novelty of experiment and the promise of success. The method was flexible and could be adapted to suit the interests of the writer, whether he was primarily an iconoclast, an analyst or a fictionist. The appeal of the mode was increased by the artistic triumph of Strachey and Maurois, as well as by the salability of the wares.

The term "the new biography" was broadly used. In the popular mind and to many critics, the biographical writing that was denominated "new" had one essential feature which distinguished it from earlier biography. This was the resemblance, real or fancied, to the characteristics of Strachey, Maurois and Ludwig. The term was applied to a diverse output which had many variations in form and substance and wide differences in quality. The books in the category were the product of all kinds of pens, and they pictured all types of figures. The term was made to embrace portraits and narratives, essays and novelizations, hypothetical arguments and psychological analyses, superficial improvisations and painstaking studies. This heterogeneous aggregate bore certain features which collectively characterized the principles and subject matter which were labeled "new."

Much of the "new biography" resulted from dissatisfaction or disgust with the old style of portraiture. The indictment of the dissenters was directed at the uncritical hero-worship of the nineteenth century. The complaint ran that men had been divested of ordinary human attributes. The whole truth about them had not been told. Lives had been written in the spirit of the Victorian epitaph. This type of veneration was obsolete when the new insurgency set in, but the revisionists of the 1920s ignored the reform which was already under way. They proceed to cut away legends which had formerly surrounded heroes and to show them with their faults and frailties. Once canonized, they were now—in a favorite word of the time—humanized. This term actually means that an author makes his characters appear like human beings. To many writers and readers it meant a revelation of faults and weaknesses, or a shift of emphasis in the portrait to those things. Some lives were written in the tone of the Spoon River epitaph. A new term, "debunk," became synonymous with the current aspect of the corrective purpose. The epithet, however, was not applicable to all the instances of revaluation.

The writers of the new school centered their attention on personality and stressed the interpretative phase of their work. Portraiture and revelation were their watchwords. They were subjective, analytic, critical. They sought motives and drew inferences and explained behavior. In some cases they wrote to support a theory or establish a thesis. They were bold exponents of the realism of the time, and they achieved a vivid actuality in their biographies. Their characters, whether drawn accurately or not, were not bookish creatures but lifelike human beings.

The "new biography" had a high degree of readability. It tended toward comparative brevity. It avoided the detailed bulk of earlier volumes and was more selective in its material. It minimized the ordinary and commonplace or excluded things of that kind from its pages. It was intended for general reading—not for special groups or for reference shelves. The "new biography" was conspicuously entertaining, picturesque and dramatic. It gave readers a new kind of vicarious experience and afforded them views of human nature which they had not seen before in life - literature. After the manner of Strachey and Maurois, the new method borrowed the illusion of reality from the novel and took pattern and design from the drama. The mode removed the boundaries between the three forms and united them for its purpose.

IV

The hazards of writing biography were greatly increased by the spread of the new practice. Revaluation of complex figures, interpretation of character and the psychological exploration of dead men's lives are clearly not an undertaking for everyone. Among those who attempted the task there were many artisans who were dexterous in manipulating the mechanics of the methods, but few artists who satisfied the spiritual demands of biography. Instead of rectifying a procedure that was faulty at the outset, the new school accepted the formula as it was and multiplied the wrongs it entailed. That much poor and superficial work should be produced under these circumstances was inevitable.

The deficiencies of the old style of the early nineteenth century were replaced by new defects. The truism that a biographer's first duty is to his figure lost force in the ebullience of the movement. The writers were frequently more intent in practising the method and striving for effect than in doing justice to their figures. The principle of selection was misused in the choice of the "marks and indications" which reveal character and illustrate personality. Plutarch had said that sometimes "the little things" about a man's manner and actions are more enlightening than great deeds and momentous events. This principle, which is valid in theory, has been abused in the twentieth century. It immediately poses two questions: What things shall be chosen to make a fair picture, and when culled and studied, what do they tell? The workers in the new style seasoned their narratives excessively with the striking, the strange, the piquant and the sensational — points that are legitimate when used in the proper proportion and relationship,—and they read convenient meanings into the ingredients of the condiment.

A serious defect was the exaggerated emphasis on weaknesses, indiscretions and improprieties. There is a ratio for blemishes as well as for merits. A wart on the nose of the subject belongs on the nose in the picture; it should not be enlarged to cover the cheek. The hero-worshippers had magnified virtues over faults; the image-breakers reversed the process. The old lack of proportion, instead of being corrected, became a frequent error in the work of the school.

The practitioners of the "new biography" were prone to use the novelist's privilege of invention. Without benefit of the necessary evidence they conjectured the thoughts which passed through men's minds at certain junctures in their lives. They devised the exact words of conversations which were held on this and that occasion. They attributed to their figures ideas and emotions which a novelist would imagine for characters of his own creation. It is one thing to present such fabrications as avowed fiction, and quite another to weave them into apparently factual narratives without due notice to the reader. To say that such figments "could" be true does not acquit them. A biographer might endow Lincoln with a dozen acts he never did or assertions he never made and still maintain a "harmony" in writing his life. The principle of sheer invention violates the law of biographical truth. Its legitimacy in fiction does not legalize its use in biography.

Of greater expedience to the biographer than the accessories of fiction were the tools of applied psychology. With these were combined the ostensible principles of psychoanalysis that are associated with Sigmund Freud. Like Strachey, Freud suffered from the inaptitude of self-styled exponents of his principles. Some of the psychologic books set forth hypotheses which were manifestly groundless or unjust, yet the conjectures were soberly termed "stimulating" and "thought-provoking" by serious readers. These volumes represented biographical speculation in one of its worst forms. The victim could not come forward to argue his case, and when no one rose to offer rebuttal, guesswork too often hardened into accepted fact.

The inadequacy of psychoanalysis as a biographical method has been summed up by Howard Mumford Jones: "In the first place, however, a Freudian interpretation of biography, to be trusted at all, must be written by one supremely competent in literature and in psychology—a rare combination. In the second place, an essential element in Freudian psychoanalysis is the uncovering of submerged memories through free association under skilful direction, but a dead man has neither memories, associations, nor the capacity to be questioned; hence it is impossible to know whether the data left behind are the really significant data. In the third place, since the interpretation of symbolism (the author's literary remains) must either rest upon, or be referred to, data gleaned from free associations, it is impossible to know whether any given interpretation is correct. In the fourth place, the selection and interpretation of symbols notoriously vary from practitioner to practitioner. In the fifth place, such interpretations are not subject to impartial controls, since the positive-negative interpretations of the analysis prevent argument as to the validity of the method, i. e., so long as any symbol can be translated into any other symbol from the subject's past, so long the psychoanalyst may roam at will, insisting upon the presence of significant symbolism when convenient, and explaining its absence, when convenient, by assuming that it has been translated into another terminology by mental censorship."[3]

V

The volume entitled *Strenuous Americans* (1923) by Roy F. Dibble illustrated the application of the Stracheyan technique by an ardent American disciple. Dedicated "To the Greatest Living Biographer," the book in its external features was a counterpart of *Eminent Victorians*. It contained sketches of seven figures: Mark Hanna, Jesse James, Frances E. Willard, Admiral George Dewey, Phineas T. Barnum, James J. Hill, and Brigham Young. These characters were

[3]"Methods in Contemporary Biography," *English Journal* (College Edition), Vol. XXI, p. 114, February 1932.

rich subjects for a pen that was using the formula of Strachey. They were strikingly individual in nature, and their
careers were filled with vivid and colorful action, which,
after being selected for the author's purpose, was further en-
livened by his gusto and enthusiasm. The paradoxes and
irreverence and irony that were suggestive of Strachey were
in the sketches, as well as his fictional features and dramatized episodes.

Zealous Americans of the type depicted in the Dibble
book were favorite subjects with biographers in the 20s.
Constance M. Rourke, who had been engaged in studying
folk customs and history in the United States, assembled a
group of nineteenth-century figures in *Trumpets of Jubilee*
(1927). Miss Rourke chose for the volume Horace Greeley,
Barnum and three members of the Beecher family, Lyman,
Henry Ward and Harriet Beecher Stowe—all of them, in
the author's metaphor, messengers of jubilation of one kind
or another. Miss Rourke's workmanship was superior to that
of Dibble. She did not use the Stracheyan formula, but her
method was a blend of the old and the new. Her biographies
were rounded and compact and were acutely executed. She
did not ridicule the oddities of her figures, but she revealed
a keen understanding of their singularities. She treated the
characters as products of the native culture. In her style
there was a strain of "the florid expansiveness" which had
been a trait of her subjects in their real lives.

M. R. Werner wrote full-length lives of Barnum (1923),
Brigham Young (1925) and Bryan (1929). Although the
books were contemporary in style and tone, Werner did not
attempt to deflate or fictionize or psychologize his characters.
He used the more conventional method of allowing them to
speak for themselves, from their utterances and writings, and
he added the necessary material and gave the whole his

interpretations. He did not exaggerate the raciness and gaiety
of Barnum's career, and he steered a temperate course
through the controversial discordances of Young's life. The
merit of the biography of Bryan depends on the attitude of
the reader toward the man. The picture drawn here is less
sympathetic and complete than the portraits of Barnum and
Young. The biography of the Mormon leader is the best of
the three books.

VI

Before 1920 the method that is termed psychological had
as a rule been used only as part of the general process of
interpretation. Biographers had not made the method their
chief means of analysis and exposition. An exception to this
rule had been Gamaliel Bradford. In the 20s the clinical
laboratory became a recognized adjunct of the "new" biographer's wookroom, and psychological autopsies were
performed with findings that were provocative and
controversial.

As a leading instrument of interpretation the psychological method has been employed in two ways. By one of them
the author attempts to prove a thesis that is involved in the
life of his figure. By the other he uses the method in making
a broad or full-length analysis of his subject. The theory behind the first way is legitimate, if the author makes his purpose clear at the outset. In trying to demonstrate his thesis,
however, the biographer may fall into certain errors. He
may — consciously or not — minimize or over-rate parts of
his data. He may ignore relevant evidence which would
weaken or destroy his proposition. He may by implication
or outright claim extend the force of his argument to cover
the whole range of his subject's life. Having begun his work

with a preconceived judgment, he must sustain his position
or admit failure. Obviously he does not choose the latter
alternative. If the biographer relies too heavily on the
psychological method by the other means of portrayal—that
of attempting to make a comprehensive examination of an
individual—he faces a limitation. The method is not all-
inclusive in its application and does not reach every aspect
of a character and career. A biographical subject is more
than a patient for clinical analysis. Dissection and diagnosis
alone do not make a complete biography. The method must
be supplemented by the expedients of conventional life-
writing if the ostensible portrait is to emerge from the status
of a case-history.

The tools that were furnished by Freud, as well as by
Jung and Adler, seemed to be providential equipment with
which to explore puzzling problems in biography. Among
these was the pessimism which Mark Twain exhibited in his
later years. Van Wyck Brooks sought the underlying reasons
of this condition. At that time Brooks believed that literary
men in the United States were forced to labor in a blighting
environment. In *The Ordeal of Mark Twain* (1920) he
examined Clemens' life by the psychoanalytic method and
attributed the humorist's state of mind and heart to the
frontier conditions in which he had grown up and to the
repressive atmosphere of his later career in the East.

Brooks used the same method to examine the voluntary
exile of a great novelist from his native country. In *The
Pilgrimage of Henry James* (1925) Brooks traced the
author's search for a congenial cultural environment. The
quest was motivated by James' discontent with a crude and
immature civilization. He sought his ideal milieu in Italy
and France, but without success, and then took up residence
in England. Here he believed at first that he had found his

goal, but the illusion turned to disappointment, and finally Henry James felt a sense of spiritual isolation from the world. In developing this theme Brooks extracted his evidence largely from James' writings and fitted the parts into a pattern which harmonized with James' life. The *Pilgrimage* is superior to *The Ordeal of Mark Twain* as an example of the psychoanalytic method.

Edgar Allan Poe has been the subject of a large amount of psychologic study. That something of a deep-seated nature was wrong with Poe has long been a common notion. His fantastic tales and strange poems, as well as the actions of his feverish career, were thought to be filled with symptoms of his malady and clues to the mystery. Workers in twentieth-century psychology and in the Freudian system in particular have shown special interest in seeking the cause of his "trouble" and the relation of the disorder to his conduct and writing. The trouble has been diagnosed with various inferences. One critic has attributed the tragedy of Poe's life "to psycho-neuroses induced by the brutal, unsympathetic treatment of his coarse and callous foster-father." A second writer has ascribed his nervous instability to "a definite lesion of one side of his brain." By another theory Poe was affected by the Oedipus complex, which he transferred successively to other women in the course of his life. To a fourth investigator the basic cause of Poe's infirmity was in effect hereditary dipsomania. Still another critic found that the reason Poe wrote at all was "a complete maladjustment to life." Perhaps Poe's unhappy condition was caused by a foreboding of what future psychological biographers would do to him.

Katharine Anthony, a pioneer worker in the psychoanalytic method, used the technique in a biography of Margaret Fuller (1920), the dynamic transcendental feminist. In the study Miss Anthony analyzed "the emotional values of an individual existence, the motivation of a career, the social transformation of a woman's energies." The work illuminated the complex realities of its heroine in a penetrating fashion. This synthesis of Margaret Fuller's contradictory qualities was a conception which emerged consistently from the figure's writings and the contemporary records.

Miss Anthony continued to specialize in the same method and made portraits of several widely different women: *Catherine the Great* (1925), *Queen Elizabeth* (1929), *Marie Antoinette* (1933), and *Louisa M. Alcott* (1938). In *The Lambs* (1945) she treated Mary and Charles together. None of these biographies was as convincing as the delineation of Margaret Fuller. The least satisfactory portrait was that of Louisa Alcott. The life of Catherine the Great suffered from lack of proportion. It read more like an embroidered psychoanalytic report on a woman with many lovers than a rounded biography of a powerful empress. None of the lives resembled a conclusive study of its heroine. Miss Anthony wrote engaging and graphic prose, she used the fruits of her extensive research easily, her portraits were original. But she carried the method to excess. With the normal function of interpretation, which she often employed effectively, she mixed conjecture and speculation.

Miss Anthony's later chronicles of Dolly Madison (1949) and Susan B. Anthony (1954) do not belong in the category of the "new biography." These lives of two widely different women are superior to the author's previous volumes. They are her best works. They do not suffer from the limitations of an overuse of the psychologic method. The portrayals have more depth and balance, and the interpretations are more firmly grounded in the data. In each biography Miss Anthony has provided a rich historical background for her character.

VII

In an iconoclastic age no historic figure was more susceptible to re-portrayal than Washington. In his case it was not
simply a matter of giving fresh interpretation to old data.
A hundred years after his death American biography still
lacked a delineation that was like the real man, complete
in all his aspects. The deeds of Washington were known,
but his full individuality, as it was actually constituted, had
never been set forth. Biography had an idealized concept
but not the living man. His features and qualities lay un-
assembled and unorganized in a vast mass of letters, diaries,
documents and other papers. The old biographers had used
these sources with due regard for the principle of *nihil nisi
bonum*. This rule meant nothing to modern investigators,
who also reaped the benefit of much new material. The
search for the true Washington which had been made by
Henry Cabot Lodge and Paul Leicester Ford was carried
forward intensively in the first half of the century. Both insurgents and more temperate biographers pursued the quest.

The authors of the 20s who made the most radical changes
in the conventional concept of Washington were William E.
Woodward and Rupert Hughes. Woodward published a life
in one volume, *George Washington: The Image and the
Man* (1926). Between 1926 and 1930 Hughes published
three volumes of a chronicle which extended from Washington's birth in 1732 to the end of the Revolution in 1781.
No later volume in this series was issued. The works of both
authors belong in the life-and-times category.

Woodward and Hughes were popular novelists who entered the craft of biography with these books. Their work
in the new field was no incidental excursion with fictional
or experimental intent. Both were violent dissenters from the

traditional view of Washington, and they set out zealously to bring "the real man" to light. They made their own independent researches without awe of their subject, respect for tradition or adherence to any school of politics. In carrying out their aim they freely exercised the privileges of the subjective biographer, interpreting their data in their own way and speaking their minds frankly.

Their philosophy of revaluation heavily affected their interpretation. In depicting Washington with faults as well as virtues both authors undoubtedly meant to be fair to their subject, but they showed a predilection for evidence that would show his uninviting qualities and trim his excellences. This bent of the biographers also appeared in their treatment of his actions and the affairs of the Revolution. The books were written in a style that was direct, brisk and matter-of-fact, but careless and unpolished. Hughes' style was the superior of the two. The same precedence may be given to his work as a whole.

In these biographies Washington was said to have been a man of stability, courage, honesty and integrity. He met "every difficulty with heroic resolution," and he possessed "saintliness unique among great soldiers and creators of nations." "He held the Revolution together by his force of character." In the course of the volumes the reader is also told that Washington married Martha Custis for her money and his real love was for Sally Fairfax. He was a shrewd speculator in Western lands. He had small vision and few ideas. He felt little faith in the masses and believed in government "by the well-born and the wealthy." He put property rights above the interests of human beings. In the midst of certain great events after the Revolution "he was principally a figure-head, a symbol." He was "the average man deified and raised to the nth power."

Woodward and Hughes, especially the latter, added a large amount of new and documented information to the general knowledge of Washington and his time. They contributed side lights on their figure which had been unknown to laymen. They also revealed the "cowardice, jealousy. dissension, graft, profiteering in almost every form and selfish indifference" with which Washington had to contend.

To judge from *Lincoln, the Man* (1931) by Edgar Lee Masters, the biographers who have found greatness in the president have misread the evidence. To Masters' view the popular Lincoln was not the true Lincoln. The myth-makers have built up a false picture. In order to correct this misconception, Masters, who disclaimed being an iconoclast, made "a rational analysis of Lincoln's mind and heart." The product of the inquiry was an invective which read like a document drawn up by Lincoln's enemies. In Masters' portrait Lincoln is presented as being stupid and mean-hearted, cruel and hypocritical, selfish and cold in his social relations, ignorant of his country and its history, incompetent as a lawyer, unprincipled as a debater, weak and pliable as an executive,—possessed of endless faults and defects. It was natural that a man of his stamp should join the Republican party. He was, however, a master of words and tender with children. Masters said that the statements in his book "are established facts, and they cannot be disputed." The facts were "interpreted" in the statements with a political animus and a strong antipathy to Lincoln as a man and a historical figure. The book would have been relished by the Copperheads in 1863. It bore the marks of a labor of hate.[4]

---

[4]Other biographies of Washington and Lincoln by authors who were not of the "new" movement are considered in Chapter XV.

VIII

The "new biography" both corrupted American life-writing and increased the vitality which already existed in the art. This vigor had appeared in the work of James Parton, and it had continued in the biographies by Paul Leicester Ford, George E. Woodberry, William Cabell Bruce and others before the 1920s. It was evident in other books of that decade which did not belong to the insurgent school. The new mode also blended technical principles of the novel and the drama with the practice of biography. The corrective aim of the dissenters was sound. That American portraits needed to be amended and amplified and rounded could not be denied. The writers of the new school, however, were not the ones to accomplish the revision, nor was the formula which they used compounded of the necessary remedial ingredients. As a result, the object of the re-interpretation was lost in the deficiencies and excesses of the school. Biographic values were transposed, the sense of obligation to the art and to the subjects was warped, and the artistic maturity which is visible in great works was lacking. The movement was at low ebb by 1932.[5]

---

[5]The books discussed in this chapter are, with the exception of Masters' *Lincoln,* representative of the "new" biography" in its better manifestations and also of the volumes which blended the new style with the traditional. Other books which are similarly typical have been omitted to avoid repetition of characteristics. Many of the biographies produced by the school have eliminated themselves from serious consideration in later years.

CHAPTER XV

BIOGRAPHY FOR THE SAKE OF BIOGRAPHY

Centuries are man-made divisions of time, but the infinite influences which affect an art know no calendar. American biography in the first half of the twentieth century was not, of course, a distinct entity which began precisely in 1900. Throughout the period the strains of its inheritance were everywhere apparent. In the broadest sense the century began with Plutarch. The example left by the Greek biographer made its "marks and indications" on the works of the most modern authors. The dicta of Samuel Johnson and the method of James Boswell were evident, as well as the signs of other men and the legacy of many things past. In a less figurative sense, if the point of beginning may be ascribed to one man, the period opened with James Parton in the preceding half-century. The biographical characteristics of the twentieth century first began to appear in well-defined form in the work of James Parton. His lives were not a full forecast of the coming period, yet they contained some of the new style that was to evolve and much of the traditional usage that was to survive.

During the first half of the twentieth century the substance of the traditional line of biography changed in two
major respects. These were the mature manifestations of
tendencies which had originated in the latter part of the
nineteenth century. In the first place, the art progressed
toward the portrayal of "the whole man" with proportionate treatment of all his traits—the uninviting with the engaging. The authors of the more impressive lives did not
agree with the older eulogists that "the faults of a good man
are but transient blemishes which quickly fade from view."
Sensitive to the logic of their art, these biographers recognized the principle that defects as well as virtues should
be included in the depiction of their figures in order to
satisfy the demands of truth. This method made their portraits more human, in the real sense of that term, and it
increased respect among laymen for honest biographical
practice. The second change was the elimination of the extraneous aims which earlier authors had adopted in re-
creating their characters. As eulogy, ethical teaching, propaganda and other encumbrances were cast off, biography
grew more "pure." These two measures of reform had a far-
reaching effect. The literature of lives reached the most advanced stage in its development when the art made deliberate effort to set forth all sides of an individual without the
burden of needless adjuncts in its subject matter.

The success of the attempt to enlarge the scope of portraiture and to purify the purpose of biography was made
possible by the cessation of a peculiar antagonism. Throughout the course of American life-literature there had been a
continual conflict between the standards of successive generations, which changed from time to time, and the absolute
canons of biography, which are constant and timeless. Biographical figures had been the center of a tug of war, as

it were, between the fashions of the age in which they were portrayed and the basic principles of truth, purity of substance and the completeness which were required by the art. It was an odd kind of conflict. It was undeclared, and to a great extent the real issue—the discrepancy in their works—was unperceived—or at least was not acknowledged—by the vast majority of biographers. One after another they proclaimed their allegiance to Truth and then obeyed the dictates of their own temperaments and the modes of their times. As long as biographers followed this custom, the progress of the art was retarded.

In the first half of the twentieth century the conflict between the shifting standards and the basic canons of biography practically ended. The dominant mood of the age, formed in large part by scientific realism, accepted the canons in both letter and spirit. The earlier nineteenth century had been anxious to praise and protect its heroes and to preserve the contemporary proprieties. The twentieth century rejected these attitudes. The age wanted the whole truth, not in a theoretical but in a practical sense. In sound and sensitive quarters during the half-century the ideals of biographical writing were acknowledged, and the canons that had long been neglected were practised with fewer reservations than before.

This state of achievement has not been universal in the field of biography. The old defects of life-writing continue to appear, but in much less frequency. Biographies are still written which give a one-sided view of their figures or are overloaded with eulogy. Not to be confounded with lives of this kind are the temperate token of tribute and the modest appreciation. Both of these types have a place in biographical literature. Books which are the media of propaganda, such as the campaign biography, are circulated at intervals.

Now and then a life composed in an obsolete style appears among the current volumes, like an ancient jalopy among modern models. With the exception of the campaign biography, "impure" biographies have greatly declined in number.

The superior biographers of the last fifty years have gone far in the quest of "the true man." If they have not brought back that visionary creature, they have made greater progress than their predecessors of previous periods, and they have achieved a record which stands out with peculiar distinction. The lustre endures in spite of the blight which the art suffered from the excesses of the 20s. Neither is the radiance of recent biography perceptibly lessened by the ever-present evils of inferior workmanship and over-production. The distinction which biography now enjoys arises from the fact that it is a fully matured art in which practice has caught up with theory. The perfect biography has not been written, but the pattern of the ideal is clear.

The best lives of the last half-century possess greater intrinsic value than the biographies of any previous period. They have a larger degree of authenticity than their predecessors. They excel in the skill and power with which they were executed. They transmit the individuality of their figures with more vitality and semblance of reality. They do more than prove that a man lived; they show him in the act of living. The recent lives, however, do not always surpass the older narratives in style.

The modern authors employed the most effective principles of contemporary practice. They retained the expedient features of classical usage and avoided the defects of the old procedure. Their works are generally free from the faults of the mode that was followed by the iconoclasts and fictionists. The more skillful practitioners of the period attained the necessary perspective which enabled them to see the facts steadily throughout the process of interpretation. Their angle of observation was a revolving view which saw all sides of the figure and examined him from without and within. When they employed the medium of psychology, they used it temperately, neither claiming too much for the science nor clothing a dubious use of it in glib words. They strived for justice for their subjects rather than for novelty of presentation. Dramatic their treatment might be, but not at the expense of the man and his record.

The authors of the superior works were exposed to the inevitable hazards of biographical writing. Being human, they were affected by the subtle agency of the personal equation. Being practitioners of an art, they could not always be calm, wholly impartial, or judicially disinterested. They were not immune to error or infallible in their judgments. In re-creating figures of the past, they could not escape an awareness of their own time. These authors, however, showed a realization of the biographer's duties and a knowledge of biographic values.

II

Biography in the twentieth century gave ample proof that a man of truly heroic stature—notably Washington, Jefferson and Lincoln—was greater than any panegyric, legend or idealization. This did not mean that the ultimate truth of these figures was reached in all respects. Evidence bearing on some circumstances remained clouded in uncertainty, judgments of judicious biographers were challenged, questionable conclusions were argued. Yet the best lives represented distinct progress toward the definitive goal. This advance was marked by an objective search for attested facts, by an insight that saw the significance of the data, and by an interpretation that made the meaning of the facts intelligible. The biographers demonstrated the greatness of their heroes by an understanding of character and achievement, by a recognition of the vicissitudes that beset the figures, and by a tolerance of their faults. These biographers, in short, accepted the men whom their best efforts brought forth and strived to re-create them in that manner.

The shortcomings of the old portraits in the nineteenth century can not be laid entirely to the eulogists, mythmakers and uncritical partisans. In many cases the authors, whatever their sympathies or antipathies, did not have sufficient material on which to draw for extensive biographies, and in other instances they did not take the time or energy to examine all the material that was available. The primary biographers of the twentieth century are tireless in their investigation and study of new material, as well as discriminating in their scrutiny of old data. The authors have also benefited from the special studies that have been made in men, movements and events. Subjects which would require months to explore are already at hand in usable form. The modern biographer, therefore, begins the writing of his book with a larger fund of material than his predecessors in the nineteenth century. Whether the process be called discovery or restoration, these biographers have made portraits of great Americans which constitute biographic reality in its most valid form.

In the second quarter of the century several authors used a broad canvas in depicting their figures. Their success with the large-scale medium dispelled the old charges that multivolume lives are ill-proportioned, filled with irrelevant material and useless minutiae, and frequently lose their characters in a maze of secondary topics: the indictment, in short, that although they may be storehouses of information, they lack art. The superior biographies of this period were free from these defects.

Although the last word on Lincoln will never be said, the biographies published between 1925 and 1955 formed a culminating stage in Lincoln research and interpretation. The authors of the several lives did not agree with one another in all their findings, nor was there unbroken acquiescence among Lincoln students in the opinions and conclusions of the biographers. Yet these authors, by their individual investigations and the collective effort of countless others, widened and deepened the area of demonstrable truth about Lincoln, and they lighted up that area by their wisdom, imagination and judgments.

William E. Barton was the author of a comprehensive biography in two parts (1925) and of several other volumes dealing with different aspects of Lincoln, such as his paternity, his lineage and his religion. Barton uncovered a mass of new evidence, he corrected errors in earlier biographies, and he exploded myths which had spiced the folklore of Lincoln. He was an expert biographical detective whose sole quarry was the fact and whose interest never flagged in any fact about Lincoln whether it was vital or trivial. Barton was a staunch realist, well endowed with common sense, objective when on the hunt, but interpreting his data by the dictates of his conscience and judgment. His zeal for his work was a conspicuous trait. Students of Lincoln at times parted company with Barton on questions of interpretation and in his conclusions. He was frank in his discussions, and he did not conceal his assurance in his biographical methods and their fruits.

Barton often fell into a personal tone with the reader and made him acquainted with the biographer's problems and difficulties. More than one reader has had the feeling of being at times a companion on the trail or a visitor to Barton's study. His style in general was diffuse and artless, unpoetic and unadorned. It was the style of an advocate presenting a factual record as he believed it to be, with infinite detail and in clear and definite terms.

Albert J. Beveridge made his biography of Lincoln (2 vols., 1928) an interpretation of the United States in Lincoln's time. Beveridge believed that "the story of a public man, to mean anything, to be truthful, or even to be entertaining, is part of the epic of the nation." Beveridge had written his life of John Marshall on this basis and had interpreted the development of American nationalism during Marshall's period. He continued the plan in the *Lincoln*. The two biographies thus became a chronicle of the national character in the first half of the nineteenth century.

In carrying out the purpose, Beveridge never neglected his central figure. The biography was an objective work prepared and written in a systematic manner. He set out to discover Lincoln among the original and authentic sources. "Facts when justly arranged interpret themselves," Beveridge said. "They tell the story." The selection of the "right" facts and their arrangement in a suitable order are two steps in objective interpretation. Beveridge applied the method rigorously. If he forbore to pass direct judgment on his hero, he was continually forced to sift the reading he did and to rule on the material he scrutinized. Thus the portrait was formed by the decisions he made and the arrangement he gave his data. It became in the end the Lincoln of Beveridge, and it was a product of critical realism, depicting "a Lincoln not so admirable and certainly not so great," but tracing "the growth, inch by inch, of a self-seeking country politician into a figure of moral grandeur and greatness."

No less effective in a proportionate degree was the biographer's treatment of the persons and happenings connected with Lincoln and the interpretation of the contemporary nationalism.

Beveridge drew heavily on Herndon's collection of material, checking the data with other testimony where it was possible. Although Beveridge rejected Herndon's "speculations and imaginings," he was generally inclined to accept what Herndon stated as facts. These were not always within the category of truth. Beveridge told the episode of Ann Rutledge with reservations, but he accepted Herndon's story of "the defaulting bridegroom."

Beveridge had planned to devote four volumes to the biography. He died soon after giving up work on the Lincoln and Douglas debates, leaving the life uncompleted in two volumes.

Under the titles of *The Prairie Years* and *The War Years* Carl Sandburg wrought a series of six volumes on Lincoln which has no counterpart in method, substance and cumulative effect. The series is like a collection of huge, well-organized dossiers containing, it would appear, everything in the world which pertained closely or remotely to Lincoln. All that he was and did, all that was felt and thought, said and written about him was, to change the figure, grist for the biographer's mill. The undertaking embraced not only a narrative of Lincoln's life and a progressive portrait of the man, but a broad background of places and affairs and the scores of individuals of every description who were in some way connected with Lincoln. The work is both personal and national history told with great masses of details, which are clear, concrete and vivid. With the central figure emerging roughly moulded from frontier clay and striving to save the Union, with the lesser characters of all ranks and occupations and purposes contributing their experiences to the march of events, *The Prairie Years* and *The War Years,* in magnitude and structure and organic whole, form a folk-like epic.

The series was published in two parts: *The Prairie Years,* issued in 1926, was in two volumes, and *The War Years,* published in 1939, comprised the remaining volumes. The six books make a continuous whole and may be treated as a unit.

Throughout the work there is a strong contemporary flavor and atmosphere. The reader sees and feels the time of Lincoln through its own collective testimony unaltered by later appraisals and evaluations. In a literal sense Sandburg let the age speak for itself out of newspapers, letters, diaries, public documents, remarks, conversations, anecdotes, editorials, speeches, sermons, memorabilia, poems, songs, cartoons, pictures—all the myriad ways in which a society in all ranks writes its autobiography. The self-chronicle is reproduced in Sandburg's pages with all its revelations of wisdom and folly, felicities and blunders, laughter and tears, crudities and refinements, hope and despair, successes and failures, virtues and villainies. The people of a period are on record here.

Sandburg was far more than a reporter of the era. He employed interpretation in various forms. He let men and affairs speak for themselves, he spoke with them, and he expressed his opinions and judgments of them. He construed his original data with his insight into its meaning and by his imaginative power and poetic suggestiveness. The work possesses enormous vitality and striking verisimilitude.

A biographical portrait that embodies the whole life of a man is an evolving characterization which changes at various phases of the figure's life. The lines and features of the portrait have their origin mainly in the words and acts of the man. The longer a biography is, the more evidence of changing character an author is able to assemble in his pages. Sandburg's delineation of the developing Lincoln is detailed and complete. All the attributes of the hero appear, and the portrait is not retouched or glossed. In *The Prairie Years* he is not the Emancipator in embryo giving signs of his destiny. The ordeal which he went through during the war is drawn with his humility, charity, shrewdness, mistakes, patience, piety, persistence, tolerance, wisdom, humor, sadness—with all the qualities which, working from a disciplinal environment, the force of events, and power of character, made the fabled "common" man into a most uncommon individual.

The last of the multi-volume chronicles of Lincoln in this group was the life by James G. Randall, a professional historian and a pre-eminent student of Lincoln. The series bore the general title of *Lincoln the President*. The first two volumes had the subtitle of *Springfield to Gettysburg* (1945), and the third volume, which dealt with the year 1863, was called *Midstream* (1952). Mr. Randall died before another volume was published. The fourth and final volume, which was completed by Richard N. Current, a colleague of Mr. Randall, was entitled *Last Full Measure* (1955).

In this work the reader has the experience of watching a skilled biographer in search of the literal truth. One does not, it is true, observe the labor of years of reading and research and the chores incidental to investigation. He does not look on the hours of study and reflection which preceded the writing of the book. The reader does, however, see the author weighing the evidence he uses, discussing the pros and cons of moot points, and analyzing the data that bears upon large topics. Part by part the biographer builds

the narrative of Lincoln's life and the historical background
into a unified whole. In his method Randall is largely objective and judicial, but he does not simply choose facts and
leave them to speak for themselves. He dissects them and
appraises their value. He pronounces judgment on men and
events, thus adding a subjectivity that is the right of a well-
grounded biographical jurist. He restates the old data which
has stood the test of his scrutiny, he revises and corrects
material that has proved to be doubtful or false, and he
adds the product of the latest research. The biography thus
has an up-to-date quality that is sustained by scholarship
and lucid expression.

The chronicler of Lincoln has a double set of problems
on his hands. He must probe, for example, the questions in
Lincoln's life such as the story of Ann Rutledge and the tale
that Mrs. Lincoln caused a "domestic hell." Both these
questions emanated from Herndon, though in the latter's
mind there was no doubt about them. Randall defended
Mrs. Lincoln against the aspersions cast on her, and he
believed that the romance of Ann Rutledge had been exaggerated. The other group of problems which confront the
biographer lie in the more numerous and complex matters
involved in the political and military affairs of Lincoln's
administrations. Here, for example, are the status of General
McClellan and the cause of the radical Republicans. Pinning
down the truth in the controversies which were kindled at
that time is an exacting task. Scholars who dissent from
some of Randall's conclusions in both categories of problems will set forth their own views. New biographers will
pore over the whole epic story, and the progression of Lincoln biographies will roll on.

III

The difficulties which confront the present-day biographer of Thomas Jefferson have become proverbial. At the outset the author undertakes to interpret a personality which had never been adequately explained. This has been caused largely by the interminable quantity of letters, documents and other papers which required examination if the investigator were to acquire a full grasp of the man. In this vast material lay an individuality that was ambiguous to some, contradictory to others, complex to all. Furthermore, partisan or adversary could each choose from Jefferson's writings and acts the parts he wanted and use them to serve his own ends. An objective attitude toward Jefferson with due regard for all sides of the man was formerly unknown. The biographies by Henry S. Randall and Parton were lacking in objectivity and completeness.

Another obstacle stood in the way of a history of Jefferson. To carry out a full portrayal, the biographer must relate to the age a many-sided man whose active interests in the culture of his time were greater than those of any other president. To perform this function successfully, the biographer must have knowledge not only of the social and political worlds in which Jefferson moved but also of the realms of intellectual, scientific and artistic things which drew his mind and heart and to which he made contributions. The author must also be cognizant of the characters and roles of Jefferson's contemporaries. A large-scale life of Jefferson, therefore, called for infinite historical and biographical knowledge and an insight into a personality which, steering clear of prejudice and distortion, would translate understanding into a faithful, progressive portrayal. The historic Jefferson came into the twentieth century without benefit of this kind of chronicle.

Such a biography is typified by *Jefferson and His Time,* a work planned for four volumes, by Dumas Malone. At this writing, two of the volumes, *Jefferson the Virginian* and *Jefferson and the Rights of Man* have been published (1948, 1951). These books comprise that part of Jefferson's life from his birth to the end of 1792. Although biographical and historical works in general are relative in their scale and finality, the volumes have essential qualities that are durable. The author's command of the objective method, the clarity of his presentation and the modest authority of his scholarship will stand, whatever interpretations of his figure are made in the future.

If Jefferson was not accorded his rightful share of biographical attention in the nineteenth century, the deficiency has been fully made up in the twentieth. Besides numerous studies in single volumes, he has been the subject of two other multi-volume works. Marie Kimball wrote a series on Jefferson with the subtitles: *The Road to Glory, 1743-1776* (1943), *War and Peace, 1776-1784* (1947), and *The Scene of Europe, 1784-1789* (1950). Claude G. Bowers, an ardent advocate of the defender of democracy, wrote three books: *Jefferson and Hamilton* (1925), *Jefferson in Power* (1936), and *The Young Jefferson, 1743-1789* (1945). The first and second of these volumes are less biographical in nature than the last.

The shelf of presidential biographies has long needed a history of James Madison which would do justice in scale and authority to the range and importance of the man's political career. Madison fathered the Constitution, he served as secretary of state under Jefferson, and he was president of his country for two terms. A career which embraced these offices obviously requires extended treatment if the associated figures and the relevant issues and events are included. The comprehensive history which Madison lacked has now been supplied by Irving Brant. At this writing four books in Brant's series of five volumes have been published: *The Virginia Revolutionist* (1941); *The Nationalist, 1780-1787* (1948), *Father of the Constitution, 1787-1800* (1950); and *Secretary of State, 1800-1809* (1953). With material drawn from original documents and first-hand sources, Brant has written a masterly biography, at the same time correcting certain misconceptions of the man and adding new knowledge of Madison's life. The portrait and personal narrative are interwoven with a detailed recital of national happenings in Madison's era. Brant writes as a vigorous advocate who is in complete command of his data and imparts its full significance to the reader. The biography is stamped with some of the best qualities of contemporary life-writing.

The longest and most authoritative biography of George Washington is the work in six volumes by Douglas Southall Freeman. The first and second books, which together are entitled *Young Washington* (1948), narrate the first twenty-seven years of the figure's life. The third and fourth volumes set forth his years as *Planter and Patriot* and as *Leader of the Revolution* (1951). The fifth volume, *Victory with the Help of France* (1952), closes with Washington's return to Mount Vernon on Christmas Eve of 1783 after he had resigned his commission before Congress. The sixth volume, *Patriot and President* (1954), embraces the later years of his public life and ends with his re-election to the presidency in March of 1793. Mr. Freeman died suddenly as he was finishing the sixth book, and the last six years of his subject's career are not recorded in the series. In these volumes the course of Washington's life is minutely unfolded in a vast setting which comprises the foreground and background from his family environment and the Virginia of his early years through the infinite and complex military and political affairs of the Revolution and the new nation.

A great asset of the work is the clear-cut rendering of primary sources, some of which had not been fully utilized. The biography keeps Washington within the limits of his own era and lacks the overtones of later tradition. It traces the growth of Washington in character and personality as that development went on, without prophecy or anticipation from the author of his subsequent experiences. Freeman adopted the method of using in the narrative only the knowledge which Washington had at particular times. This method tends to sharpen the re-creation of the hero, but it excludes information which would round out given situations in the mind of the reader. The complete portrait—minus the last years of Washington's life—is a balanced treatment of his virtues and non-virtues. Although Washington is interpreted from the data of his own time, rather than from the viewpoints of later generations, judgments were necessary, and Freeman, with his mastery of the material, was in an expedient position to make them. The biographer pursues his task in the manner of a fair-minded judge who tries to rule equitably on the evidence. He corrects and supplements earlier lives of his figure with sound testimony. He shows, for instance, that Washington could be emotional, impetuous and aggressive on occasion, and that his mother did not exert on him the influence which appears in tradition. The biography has been criticised adversely on the ground that it lacks proportion in certain of its parts and that it contains irrelevant matter.*

---

*American biography suffered a great loss in the deaths of Albert J. Beveridge. James G. Randall and Douglas S. Freeman while they were engaged on their multi-volume works. There is, of course, no lack of information about the years of their subjects' lives which they left unrecorded, but we do not have those years in the words of these biographers.

Broad as the preceding panoramic biographies are in range and bulk, and intricate in pattern, they exhibit the same proficiency in technical principles that appear in the best one-volume lives. Although the amount of history which a biography of this type should contain is always a moot point, the authors of these books have blended the portrayal of the protagonists and the pertinent events and public questions without awkwardness or confusion. They have lighted up the private sides of their figures with concrete details and anecdotes. Despite the magnitude of these works the books need not be taken up by the reader from a sense of duty or with an air of resignation; they richly repay the close attention they entail. A biographer who spends years with a magnetic figure risks being "captured" by the object of his devotion. If these authors have been captured in that sense, they have in turn mastered in surpassing degree the individuality of their heroes and the welter of events through which the men rose to biographical importance.

IV

Among the biographies written in one and two volumes in this period there are variant forms of the usual method of presentation.

In the final phase of subjective interpretation an author gives his data his conception of its meaning and significance. At the end of the biography the reader has a finished picture before him. *The Melville Log* (1951) by Jay Leyda is a departure from the conventional style of portraiture. In two volumes which comprise almost a thousand pages, Mr. Leyda provides the reader with a vast collection of materials from which "to be his own biographer" and "build his own approach to the complex figure." The data is arranged in the chronological order "through as many of Melville's days as could be restored, so that the reader may watch him as he works, sees, reacts, worries." Mr. Leyda extracted the entries from the novelist's writings and a wide variety of contemporary records, and he put them together without thesis, applause or prejudice. Herman Melville is thus seen developing and changing in the setting of his own time without the intrusion of later appraisals and criticism. *The Melville Log* is a unique addition to the shelf of books on Melville and an authoritative corrective to some of those volumes.

Marchette Chute in her *Shakespeare of London* (1949) likewise restricts her data to the period in which her subject lived. The book is composed in the conventional form of the running narrative and finished portrait. She "used no evidence dated later than 1635." In setting Shakespeare's career as a whole "against the background of his own day" Miss Chute followed a common practice in biography, but unlike many authors she did not look forward beyond that background and reflect the judgments of future generations. She shows Shakespeare "as his contemporaries saw him rather than as the gigantic and legendary figure he has since become." The biography "concerns only that part of him that was mortal and belonged to the Elizabethan age. His works are not discussed as literature but only as they relate to the working problems of the London stage." (From the Foreword) Miss Chute's method, which she used with marked success, heightens the reality of her figure and gives her book a special value among the lives of Shakespeare.

The Lincoln Reader (1947) differs from the conventional biography in the multiplicity of its authorship. The contents of the volume consist of 179 selections drawn from the writings of 65 individuals and "arranged to form an integrated narrative." The editor, Paul M. Angle, does not claim that the selections are the "best" work of the writers who are represented; he has "simply taken from each author what seemed to fit best at a given point in the book—a fine piece of narrative here, a vivid reminiscence there, a penetrating character study or a contemporary diary entry at other places." The contributors include not only professional biographers of the last seventy-five years, but also Lincoln himself and men who had firsthand information of particular phases and happenings in his life. A book of this kind, to be successful as a biography, obviously requires a thorough knowledge of Lincolnana and an exact sense of discrimination. Mr. Angle has also knit the selections together skillfully and supplied connecting notes and explanations which enable the reader to move easily from part to part. A feature of the anthology is that the reader sees Lincoln from numerous points of view. This is an advantage or a drawback, according to his taste. *The Lincoln Reader* brings out with singular clarity what Lincoln was and did in his own time. In achieving that goal it shows essentially what he means today.

V

In concluding a lecture on the art of biography in 1920, William Roscoe Thayer remarked that the foremost trait of the form at that time seemed to be its multiplicity. A similar observation had been made by Jared Sparks in 1818, and the same comment recurred periodically in subsequent years. The steady abundance of fiction has been taken for granted by critics and laymen, but the profusion of biography has been pointed out as a phenomenon in every generation. The multiplicity of production to which Thayer referred continued with fluctuations from 1920 to 1955. Within the limits of those years approximately 20,835 biographies were published in the United States. Its multiplicity has been the most obvious and the least significant aspect of American biography.

Far more striking and important than the size of the output is the high proportion of superior lives. If a skeptic alleges that propinquity lends undue enchantment to these books, the standards of the art quickly refute the notion by the undazzled judgment which they render on the workmanship and validity of the biographies. Carlyle's statement that a well-written life was almost as rare as a well-spent one loses its present force before the weight of this evidence.

In this chapter the state of American biography in the first half of the twentieth century has been defined, and the main principles which governed the art have been outlined and illustrated in the several lives of the presidents. There remain a great number of recent biographies which possess the marks of distinction. To consider each one of these books would expand the present treatment to the length of an annotated bibliography. To consider many of them separately would mean repetition of the same philosophical and technical principles which have been described in the present chapter and in other parts of this volume. A selective list of the biographies published from 1920 to 1955 is given in Appendix A.

The recent books represent the culmination of a development which began in this country with the "morsel of biography" by John Norton. During the course of its growth American life-literature has evolved in changing patterns and various forms. The complete roll of its characters is the dramatis personae of every field of activity. From one point of view the American heritage is illustrated in the written lives of its makers.

In the main line of its development biography passed through the stages of the memorial, the monument of uncritical hero-worship, and the mirror of the proprieties. Each of these stages had its superior books, and the course of native life-writing was advanced in each stage. When the art came to practise the basic principles with a critical realism and rational interpretation, it reached another stage and gave a complete portrayal of its characters without extraneous admixture and trappings. Future generations will write their own biographies and draw their own conclusions. If the record of the past is prophetic, viewpoints will change, emphases will shift, different interpretations will be made. Whatever the future mutations are, they can not destroy the achievements of the best lives of the first half of the twentieth century that were written for the simplest and greatest reason of all—for the sake of biography.

APPENDIXES

APPENDIX A

SELECTIVE LIST OF BIOGRAPHIES, 1920-1955

In the following list of biographies published between 1920 and 1955, the aim has been to combine effective portrayal with a certain degree of variety of figures in a comparatively short number of books. The list obviously does not contain all the superior biographies published within those years. Neither have merit and diversity of figures been exhausted here.

As a rule only full-length biographies have been included, although exceptions have been made in books like *Captain Sam Grant* by Lloyd Lewis and *Sam Clemens of Hannibal* by Dixon Wecter. In the case of multi-volume biographies which are in the process of being written, the number of volumes already published has not been given for the reason that these are constantly subject to change until the sets are completed. Certain books published before 1920, as the *Life of Albert Gallatin* by Henry Adams, have been included, with the dates of publication, where it seemed desirable, in order to round out the plan of the list. In the list the names of the figures portrayed, not necessarily the titles of the books, are given.

Much longer bibliographies are in the volume *Biography by Americans* 1658-1936 (published 1939) by Edward H. O'Neill and the *Harvard Guide to American History* (1954). Numerous other bibliographies of varying length are also available. The *Dictionary of American Biography* is the standard collection of short and condensed biographies.

ABIGAIL ADAMS.   Janet Whitney

HENRY ADAMS.   Elizabeth Stevenson

JOHN ADAMS.   Catherine Drinker Bowen

JOHN QUINCY ADAMS.   Bennett Champ Clark

SAMUEL ADAMS.   John C. Miller

LOUIS AGASSIZ *(Runner of the Mountain Tops)*.   Mabel L. Robinson

AMOS BRONSON ALCOTT *(Pedlar's Progress)*. Odell Shepard

LOUISA M. ALCOTT.   Madeleine B. Stern

JOHN PETER ALTGELD *("Eagle Forgotten")*.   Harry Barnard

SUSAN B. ANTHONY.   Katharine Anthony

JOAN OF ARC.   Albert Bigelow Paine

BENEDICT ARNOLD.   Charles C. Sellers

JOHN J. AUDUBON.   Francis H. Herrick (1917)
———————— Constance Rourke

LUDWIG VAN BEETHOVEN.   Alexander W. Thayer

ALBERT J. BEVERIDGE *(Beveridge and the Progressive Era)*.   Claude G. Bowers

NAPOLEON BONAPARTE.   James M. Thompson (The author is an English historian.)

DANIEL BOONE.   John Bakeless

EDWIN BOOTH *(Prince of Players)*. Eleanor Ruggles

LOUIS D. BRANDEIS.   Alpheus T. Mason

JOHN BROWN.   Oswald Garrison Villard (1910)

JOHN C. CALHOUN.   Margaret L. Coit
———————— Charles M. Wiltse

CAMILLO BENSO CAVOUR.   William Roscoe Thayer (1911)

HENRY CLAY.   Glyndon G. Van Deusen

SAMUEL L. CLEMENS *(Sam Clemens of Hannibal)*.   Dixon
   Wecter
——————— DeLancey Ferguson
——————— Albert Bigelow Paine
GROVER CLEVELAND.   Allan Nevins
CHRISTOPHER COLUMBUS.   Samuel E. Morison
DAVID CROCKETT.   Constance Rourke
HARVEY CUSHING.   John F. Fulton
EUGENE V. DEBS *(The Bending Cross)*.   Ray Ginger
CHARLES DICKENS.   Edgar Johnson
EMILY DICKINSON.   Thomas H. Johnson
——————— *(This Was a Poet)*.   George F. Whicher
THEODORE DREISER.   F. O. Matthiessen
JONATHAN EDWARDS.   Ola E. Winslow
CHARLES W. ELIOT.   Henry James
RALPH WALDO EMERSON.   Ralph L. Rusk
F. SCOTT FITZGERALD.   Arthur Mizener
HENRY FORD.   Allan Nevins
——————— Keith Sward
BENJAMIN FRANKLIN.   Carl Van Doren
SIGMUND FREUD.   Ernest Jones
——————— Helen Walker Puner
MARGARET FULLER.   Mason Wade
ALBERT GALLATIN.   Henry Adams (1879)
HENRY GEORGE.   Charles A. Barker
ULYSSES S. GRANT *(Captain Sam Grant)*.   Lloyd Lewis
——————— Bruce Catton
HORACE GREELEY.   Glyndon G. Van Deusen
ALEXANDER HAMILTON.   Nathan Schachner
NATHANIEL HAWTHORNE.   Newton Arvin
——————— Randall Stewart
PATRICK HENRY.   Jacob Axelrod
WILLIAM H. HERNDON.   David Donald
SIDNEY HILLMAN.   Matthew Josephson
OLIVER WENDELL HOLMES (SR.) *(Holmes of the Breakfast
   Table)*.   M. A. DeWolfe Howe
——————— Eleanor M. Tilton

OLIVER WENDELL HOLMES (JR.) *(Yankee from Olympus)*.
    Catherine Drinker Bowen
SAM HOUSTON *(The Raven)*. Marquis James
CHARLES E. HUGHES. Merlo J. Pusey.
WASHINGTON IRVING. Stanley T. Williams
ANDREW JACKSON. John Spencer Bassett
———————— Marquis James
———————— John W. Ward
HENRY JAMES *(The Untried Years, 1843-1870)*.   Leon
    Edel
———————— F. W. Dupee
WILLIAM JAMES. Ralph Barton Perry
JAMES FAMILY. F. O. Matthiessen
THOMAS JEFFERSON. Gilbert Chinard
———————— Marie Kimball
———————— Dumas Malone
———————— Nathan Schachner
SAMUEL JOHNSON *(Young Sam Johnson)*.   James L.
    Clifford
———————— Joseph Wood Krutch
MARQUIS DE LAFAYETTE. Louis R. Gottschalk
———————— Brand Whitlock
ABRAHAM LINCOLN. James G. Randall
———————— Carl Sandburg
———————— Nathaniel W. Stephenson
———————— Benjamin P. Thomas
MARY TODD LINCOLN. Ruth Painter Randall
ROBERT E. LEE. Douglas S. Freeman
———————— Robert W. Winston
LOWELLS AND THEIR SEVEN WORLDS. Ferris Greenslet
IGNATIUS DE LOYOLA. Henry D. Sedgwick
JAMES MADISON. Irving Brant
JOHN MARSHALL. Albert J. Beveridge (1916-19)
PETER MARSHALL *(A Man Called Peter)*. Catherine Wood
    Marshall
INCREASE MATHER. Kenneth B. Murdock

Guy de Maupassant.   Ernest A. Boyd
Mayo Brothers.   Helen Clapesattle
Cyrus Hall McCormick.   William T. Hutchinson
Herman Melville.   Newton Arvin
———————— Leon Howard
Sir William Osler.   Harvey Cushing
Thomas Paine.   Moncure D. Conway (1892)
Theodore Parker.   Henry Steele Commager
Francis Parkman.   Mason Wade
Louis Pasteur.   Rene J. Dubos
Franklin Pierce.   Roy F. Nichols
Edgar Allan Poe.   Hervey Allen
———————— Arthur Hobson Quinn
———————— George E. Woodberry
Ernie Pyle.   Lee G. Miller
Henry J. Raymond.   Francis Brown
Paul Revere.   Esther Forbes
John D. Rockefeller.   Allan Nevins
Franklin D. Roosevelt.   Frank Freidel
Theodore Roosevelt.   Henry F. Pringle
Elihu Root.   Philip C. Jessup
Jean Jacques Rousseau.   Matthew Josephson
William Shakespeare.   Joseph Q. Adams
———————— Marchette Chute
Percy Bysshe Shelley.   Newman I. White
William T. Sherman.   Lloyd Lewis
Joseph Smith (*No Man Knows My Story*).   Fawn Brodie
Robert Louis Stevenson.   J. C. Furnas
Mary Stuart.   Herbert S. Gorman
Henry David Thoreau.   Joseph Wood Krutch
Ivan Turgenev.   Avraham Yarmolinsky
Booker T. Washington.   Samuel R. Spencer, Jr.
George Washington.   John C. Fitzpatrick
———————— Douglas S. Freeman
Daniel Webster.   Claude M. Fuess
William H. Welch.   Simon and James T. Flexner

WALT WHITMAN.   Gay W. Allen
JOHN G. WHITTIER.   John A. Pollard
WOODROW WILSON.   Ray Stannard Baker
———————   H. C. F. Bell
———————   Arthur S. Link
ÉMILE ZOLA.   Matthew Josephson

APPENDIX B

A NOTE ON CAMPAIGN BIOGRAPHIES

Biography has long been used as a political instrument in national elections. Since the early nineteenth century American voters have periodically been showered with pamphlets and books in the form of "campaign lives," which were issued to inform and persuade them in the choice of their next president.

The first accounts of this kind are usually published months before the nominations are made. When a man in the public eye has acquired the stature of a potential candidate for the presidency, some discerning writer believes that the open secret should no longer be kept from the electorate, and especially from those individuals who are more actively interested in the selection of a party nominee. The writer in question accordingly composes an account of the man's life and achievements, and he makes it plain in point-blank or oblique fashion that his subject would be a desirable candidate in the next campaign.

The biographies that go straight to their purpose are published after the delegates in convention have made their

nominations for president and vice president. Voters of all
parties must be informed about the nominees, and skillful
pens go to work for the candidates with vigor and enthusiasm. There is no obliqueness or subtlety in the method of
these biographies. They are thoroughgoing pieces of campaign literature.

For over one hundred years the campaign biography has
been a recognized document in the storm and stress of national elections. A presidential contest without its sanguine
biographies of ideal candidates would be like a travel tour
with no glowing prospectus of blissful sight-seeing. The campaign biography which emerges from tradition is a symbol
of flowery rhetoric, extravagant claims and aspirants for
office who were paragons of human virtues and statesman-
ship. This formula, however, has not been universal to the
type. Many campaign lives have been written with restraint
and moderation. A few of them have even opposed, if not
derided, the candidates they professed to portray.

II

The biography in book and pamphlet form grew into use
as an instrument of political literature in the 1820s, when
Andrew Jackson, robust representative of the growing
democracy, was a candidate for president. The picturesque
soldier had engaged a biographer's attention soon after his
exploits in the War of 1812. His whole career offered a
dramatic story for popular reading. The narrative was begun by Major John Reid, who had been aide to Jackson
in the operations at New Orleans, and was finished, after
the death of Reid, by John H. Eaton, senator from Tennessee, and a future member of Jackson's cabinet. The biography was first published in Philadelphia in 1817, six years
before Jackson was a presidential candidate.

When he was nominated by many sectional conventions in 1823 and 1824, before the dawn of national conventions, his friends felt that his fortunes would be advanced by republication of the Eaton book, and it was issued again in 1824. Although its hero was defeated in the election, which was thrown into the House of Representatives, the book had opposed "the torrent of abuse which was poured on General Jackson," and it strengthened his reputation among the rank and file of the voters. When Old Hickory was again a candidate—and a successful one—in 1828, other writers brought out new accounts of his life which were extensively circulated. Its usefulness once demonstrated, the campaign biography continued to multiply in succeeding presidential contests.

The early biographies did not always praise the figures they portrayed. In some cases they attacked their subjects. A work of the negative kind came forth in the bitter fight between the Jackson and anti-Jackson forces in 1836. The book, which was both novel and vituperative, was a life of Martin Van Buren, whom Jackson desired to be his successor in the White House. The title-page bore as the author the name of David Crockett, who, while a member of Congress from Tennessee, had broken with Jackson and aligned himself with the Whigs. Crockett probably did not write all the biography and perhaps not any part of it. His professed authorship was intended to have weight among the Jacksonians. The book assailed the "heir apparent to the government' " in coarse language.

On the title-page was the verse:
"Good Lord! what is Van!—for though simple he looks,
Tis a task to unravel his looks and his crooks;
With all his depths and his shallows, his good and his evil,
All in all, he's a Riddle must puzzle the devil."

The author, however, had no difficulty in solving the enigma with satanic spleen. He called Van Buren "a Dandy," and said that his subject "is laced up in corsets such as women in town wear, and if possible tighter than the best of them." He fathomed the candidate's mental processes with the explanation that "his mind beats round, like a tame bear tied to a stake, in a little circle, hardly bigger than the circumference of the head in which it is placed." Anticipating the allegation that he had not written the book, Crockett protested at the end: "No, no, people must not think that because Me and General Jackson had no education and came from nothing, we can't write."

In contrast to this fantastic outpouring, sympathetic biographies of the conventional kind appeared to uphold Van Buren and support the principles of his party.

In the canvass of 1852 the Democrats through the country found that the author of *The Scarlet Letter* had taken up his pen in behalf of their candidate. The role of political biographer was a strange part for Nathaniel Hawthorne, and only his personal friendship with Franklin Pierce led him to write a life of the nominee from New Hampshire. In a letter congratulating Pierce on his nomination, Hawthorne offered his services to his old college comrade and mentioned "the necessary biography," but he added his belief that other men could do a better piece of work of that kind. "It needs long thought with me, in order to produce anything good," Hawthorne wrote.

Pierce took a different view of the matter. Before receiving the letter he had had Hawthorne in mind for a campaign life, though other biographies of him were already under way, and he finally induced his friend to make the portrait. He knew that Hawthorne would turn out a good book, and he did not forget the effect of the novelist's reputation. *The Scarlet Letter* and *The House of the Seven Gables* had been published within three years of his nomination.

Hawthorne finished the book — a rapid production — in the summer of 1852. In the preface he said frankly that he "would not voluntarily have undertaken the work," but that in the present event a friend "should be sketched by one who has had opportunities of knowing him well, and who is certainly inclined to tell the truth." Hawthorne was not unduly swayed by his personal connection with Pierce. The biography was not adorned with garlands of rhetorical laurel. It was naturally favorable to its subject, but was marked by moderation and restraint. The life of Pierce was a bit of task-work by a sensitive artist who turned for the moment from his own field to do an act of friendship.

Eight separate biographies of Lincoln were published in English during the campaign of 1860. Three — at least — political biographies in German were issued in the same year. There were a large number of German voters among the electorate, especially in Illinois.

The biography which is now the most remembered, on account of the author's later eminence, was that written by William Dean Howells. At the time Howells was twenty-three years old and held the position of professional reader for a publisher in Columbus, Ohio. His employer planned to issue a campaign life of the Republican nominee and wished Howells to compile it. The young man was averse to going to Springfield to interview Lincoln, and a young law student was sent to get the material for him.

The notes were brought back to him, and Howells, feeling at home with the material which belonged to his native region, wrote "a hurried book." It was temperate in tone, and the author did not conclude his narrative with the con-

ventional prophecy of his figure's election. Instead, "he
prefers to leave the future of Lincoln to Providence and to
the people." Howells said in later years that he never
learned what Lincoln thought of the book.

III

From Lincoln to the present time, "the necessary biography," as Hawthorne had called it, has appeared as regu-
larly as keynote speeches, visits of notification committees
and last-minute predictions of party managers. Biographers
have drawn their figures in language that has ranged from
mild praise to extreme flattery. Some writers have admitted
that their heroes had faults, but the defects have been minimized or metamorphosed into seeming merits. The weaknesses, if they have been allowed to exist, have been over-
shadowed by great characteristics. The style of the campaign biographies has changed from time to time, as fashions
in general life-writing have altered. The high-flown phrases
of earlier biographies have given way to less ornate diction,
and the lavish panegyric has become as rare as the Victorian obituary. Whatever their mode of expression, however, the campaign biographers have never forgotten their
all-important purpose. The individual volumes have circulated for their brief season and disappeared, but the campaign biography as a type has held its place through the rise
and fall of candidates and parties. When the political sun
shines on the nominees, many a loyal biographer comes to
the aid of his candidate.

APPENDIX C

A NOTE ON ROGUE AND CRIMINAL BIOGRAPHIES

At the beginning of the eighteenth century the incipient American biography consisted of a small group of clerical memoirs and the collection of lives written by Cotton Mather. As the century advanced, strange characters began to appear among this respectable company of worthies. The new figures were rogues and criminals, and in odd contrast to their law-abiding predecessors of the memoirs they attained the biographical status by reason of their transgressions against society. The wrongdoers were fertile subjects for writers who aimed to teach or to entertain or to combine those purposes. If the bad men died on the gallows or met another ignominious end, they could be held up as object lessons of the wages of sin. If they reformed in their way of living, the moral of their misdeeds was still pertinent and might be heightened with words of warning from the professed penitents. Furthermore, the careers of the wayward offered diverting narratives even when the writer kept to the truth; but when the lives were embroidered by imaginative pens, the tales were all the more fascinating. The makers of the crime lore knew well the sweet uses of evil-doing.

The earliest pieces of this criminal literature were crude ballads and doggerel, which were circulated on broadsides. These were followed by short sketches in prose and condensed narratives, which were printed in pamphlet form. The actual authorship of the accounts was seldom made known. Ghost-writers, who were usually self-chosen, composed many of the sketches and narratives. In some cases, while retaining their anonymity, they acknowledged their part in the accounts. In other instances the narratives were published as solely the work of the culprit himself. The condemned man, it was often alleged, had written out his own story or had dictated his confession before going to the gallows.

The ballads dwelt on the crimes and execution of the felons and touched briefly on a few other happenings in their careers. In the prose accounts the readers were treated to more realistic details of fact and fiction. No one was more alive to the tastes of their clients than these American Defoes, but their style was in the mode of the time. They could not anticipate the tactics of future purveyors of crime. For sensational devices the printers resorted to capital letters, exclamation points and rude representations of convicts in cells and murderers awaiting the noose on the gallows.

The final chapter of crime and conviction was frequently the gallows sermon. This was delivered in church or near the base of the gibbet, and in the discourse the preacher reviewed the wickedness of the life which was about to end. The lesson of the sermon was a strong antidote for the tale of earthly iniquity, and the fate of the sinner was forcefully portrayed to the congregation or to the crowd which was gathered for the execution. The gallows sermon did not perish with its delivery on that occasion. It was printed and circulated as a tract. The sermon was often published with a sketch of the criminal's life.

Representative of the criminal pamphlets is the short sketch of one Joseph Andrews, who was tried and put to death for piracy and murder, in New York in 1769. Andrews made a confession "to the gentlemen of the clergy who visited him during his confinement and to the keepers of the gaol the day before his execution," and he told them the circumstances of his life. To this were added further details of his trial and execution. The narrative of Samuel Brand, who was hanged for the murder of his brother, at Lancaster, Pennsylvania, was set forth in "a succinct account of his person, parentage, principles and temper, interspersed with some interesting reflections, moral and religious." (1774). The execution of Caleb Adams for murder, at Windham, Connecticut, in 1803 was immediately followed by the publication of a pamphlet which contained "a sketch of the circumstances of the birth, education and manner of Caleb's life." With the sketch was the sermon preached at the time he was hanged and an appendix which gave an "account of the behavior of the criminal at his trial, during confinement and on the day of execution."

In the class of rogue and criminal autobiographies, real or purported, three narratives of extended length survived their time and have been published in later editions. They are *Memoirs of the Notorious Stephen Burroughs* (2 vols., 1798, 1804), *A Narrative of the Life, Adventures, Travels and Sufferings of Henry Tufts* (1807), and *A Narrative of the Life and Adventures of Captain Lightfoot* (1821).

Rogues and criminals have continued to draw the interest of biographic writers since the early eighteenth century. The rogue has received much less attention than the felon. Like the biographies of individuals who enjoyed a reputable

standing in society, the life-narratives of this class changed
in their features from time to time. The gallows sermon soon
disappeared as an adjunct to the pamphlet stories for the
reason that the formal discourse was no longer given at the
execution. In one form or another, the "moral and religious
reflections" on the life and wickedness of the evil-doer lasted
well into the nineteenth century. The pointed lesson was a
natural concomitant in an age that believed in the didactic
value of literature. The "moral" also served on occasion to
ease the conscience of both the purveyor of a shocking tale
and the reader who feasted on it. Some writers waxed sentimental in mild or mawkish fashion over the misspent lives
of their subjects and offered palliating circumstances for the
wrongs the culprits had done. In the twentieth century the
realistic criminal biography, devoid of lesson and sentiment,
has been numerous. The habitual bad man has always been
"good copy," especially if his exploits had been well
advertised before the biographic writer took him up.

INDEX

INDEX

Biographies are indicated by the italicized names of their subjects.

The biographies in Appendix A, which are listed in the alphabetical order, are not included in the Index unless they appear in other parts of the book.

INDEX

INDEX

INDEX

INDEX

INDEX

INDEX

INDEX

INDEX